No Longer Aliens,
No Longer Strangers

South Florida-Rochester-Saint Louis
Studies on Religion and the Social Order
EDITED BY

Jacob Neusner   William Scott Green   William M. Shea

NO LONGER ALIENS, NO LONGER STRANGERS
Christian Faith and Ethics for Today

by
A. Roy Eckardt

No Longer Aliens, No Longer Strangers

Christian Faith and Ethics for Today

A. Roy Eckardt

Scholars Press
Atlanta, Georgia

NO LONGER ALIENS, NO LONGER STRANGERS
Christian Faith and Ethics for Today
by
A. Roy Eckardt

Published by Scholars Press
for the University of South Florida, University of Rochester,
and Saint Louis University

Library of Congress Cataloging in Publication Data
Eckardt, A. Roy (Arthur Roy), 1918-
    No longer aliens, no longer strangers : Christian faith and ethics
for today ; A. Roy Eckardt.
        p.   cm. — (South Florida-Rochester-Saint Louis studies on
religion and the social order ; v. 9)
    Includes bibliographical references and indexes.
    ISBN 1-55540-999-7 (cloth). — ISBN 0-7885-0000-7 (pbk.)
    1. Man (Christian theology) 2. Faith. 3. Christian ethics.
I. Title. II. Series.
BT701.2.E28   1994
233—dc20   94-25965
                                   CIP

Printed in the United States of America
on acid-free paper

For My Colleagues in

The Christian Scholars Group on

Judaism and the Jewish People

For not of thy will wast thou formed and not of thy will dost thou die, and not of thy will art thou to give just account and reckoning before the King of the kings of the kings, the Holy One, Blessed be He.

Pirke Aboth, IV.29

To believe in God means to understand the question about the meaning of life. To believe in God means to see that the facts of the world are not the end of the matter. To believe in God means to see that life has a meaning.

Ludwig Wittgenstein

Mysticism without politics becomes mystification. Politics without awe of the holy becomes cynical and tired.

Joseph C. Williamson

You have sorrow now, but your hearts will rejoice, and no one will take your joy from you.

John 16:22

CONTENTS

Preface

I share a wish many writers have that their readers will respond to a given book as an integral element within their developing work in its entirety. That wish may often be unrealistic and sometimes presumptuous, but the hope is still there.

I dedicate this particular effort to Protestant and Catholic colleagues in the Christian Scholars Group on Judaism and the Jewish People, in thanksgiving for their acceptance of me and their criticisms of me over almost a quarter of a century. Elements in the present little book reflect their influence upon me. "Their" includes my wife Alice Eliza, a particularly lively and creative member of that ongoing seminar.

Unless otherwise noted, biblical citations in this book are from the New Revised Standard Version.

A. ROY ECKARDT

Lehigh University
Bethlehem, Pennsylvania
United States
and
Centre for Hebrew and Jewish Studies
University of Oxford
United Kingdom

1

Beginnings

Along the theological and moral road I have been traveling for some time, I seek to mediate between historic truths of the Christian tradition and the responsibilities of contemporary life. Yet such a mediating journey is anything but original or peculiar to me. It may even be a prevailing outlook these says – and hence not entirely safe from what Paul Ricoeur calls a "hermeneutics of suspicion." Jaroslav Pelikan somewhere distinguishes between traditionalism as a dead faith of living people and tradition as a living faith of dead people. Believers alive today may help keep a tradition alive and also help shape its course.

This book is a brief enchiridion of certain salient, essential elements in Christian faith and life: the Christian understanding of the nature of humankind and its place in the world; what it means to speak of and belong to the church; the person and activity of God, with special reference to God's work in Jesus Christ; standards and principles that govern Christian morality; a (limited) number of specific applications of the Christian ethic to daily living; the quality of Christian humor; and reflections upon death and eternal life.[1]

Part One of the book concentrates upon Christian anthropology and theology (chapters 2-5). Part Two seeks to reckon with Christian moral responsibility (chapters 6-7). Part Three concerns itself with two distinctive elements in Christian faith: Humor and comedy; and death and eternal life (chapters 8-9). The three parts of my study

---

[1]Peter Steinfels has an interesting reminder: "Theologians have long recognized that some church teachings, although duly proclaimed, were simply never 'received' by the faithful – and eventually fell into disuse" ("The Anglicans' Non-Universal Church," *The New York Times*, 14 August 1988).

are interrelated, since I interpret the Christian faith as leading naturally into the Christian ethic, and the Christian ethic as grounded essentially upon the Christian faith.

The book is a modest sequel to two fairly substantial volumes of mine, *For Righteousness' Sake* and *Reclaiming the Jesus of History*. Big books run the risk of either belaboring their subject or consuming large amounts of reader time. Yet little books are prey to undue simplification. (I once heard an editor's delightful remedy for this dilemma. A good book is 224 pages long.) In any case, I think there is a place for relatively short exercises such as this one. I hope that my fairly extensive notes and references within each chapter together with the bibliography "For Further Reading" will not be passed over but will be treated as integral to the whole and as providing means for the reader to expand the operation on her or his terms.[2]

Objectivity and Commitment

The main thing I want to do by way of getting us started is to offer some thoughts upon the lingering argument over objectivity and commitment in religious and theological writing, including an indication of where I am coming from in this respect.

Sallie McFague expresses worry over the systematicians who "were usually 'solo' players, each concerned to write his (the 'hers' were in short supply) magnum opus . . . . As the deconstructionists have underscored, these theologians also strove to assert, against different voices, the *one* voice (their own – or at least the voice of their own kind) as *the* truth, the 'universal' truth."[3] Ellen T. Chary

---

[2]In other writings I have sought to be more intensive and extensive respecting Christian teachings: On Christology, *Reclaiming the Jesus of History* (Minneapolis: Fortress Press, 1992); on the neglected subject of the Devil, *How To Tell God From the Devil* (forthcoming); on liberation thinking (dealing with racism, sexism, and antisemitism), *Black-Woman-Jew* (Bloomington: Indiana University Press, 1989); on Christian moral philosophy, *For Righteousness' Sake* (Bloomington: Indiana University Press, 1987); on humor, *Sitting in the Earth and Laughing* (New Brunswick-London: Transaction Publishers, 1992); and on Christian-Jewish relations, *Jews and Christians* (Bloomington: Indiana University Press, 1986), including discussion of religion and the public order, and (the sexist-titled) *Elder and Younger Brothers* (New York: Charles Scribner's Sons, 1967; Schocken Books, 1973).
[3]Sallie McFague, "An Earthly Theological Agenda," *The Christian Century* 108 (1991): 13. Aware though I am of McFague's criticism, I do not quite have the heart to jettison the following list of systematic works: See, e.g., Francis Schüssler Fiorenza and John P. Galvin, eds., *Systematic Theology: Roman Catholic Perspectives*, 2 vols. (Minneapolis: Fortress Press, 1991); Hans Küng, *On Being A Christian*, trans. Edward Quinn (New York: Pocket Books, 1976);

rightly (I think) objects to a trend in our time to turn the exigencies of the individual into a sort of theological authority. She laments a cult of personal experience that is rather fashionable in recent theological and ethical writing.[4]

I can offer no final resolution of the difficult question of subjectivity versus objectivity, but I do have two pertinent suggestions.

> 1. It is essential that we be as forthright and honest as we can and make clear our personal situation and viewpoint so that others may be on proper guard – or, for that matter, may derive proper benefit. The present exposition is conditioned by my being a white, gentile, middle-class, Protestant (United Methodist) American male earthling who is living – and dying (a "sojourner on the way to death"[5]) – in the waning years of the twentieth century. (I have more to say below respecting my theological presuppositions.)

> 2. Christianity, I should argue, is not something restrictedly "true for me," but is rather something primarily "true for us," the Christian community of faith. In this regard the church reminds us of the long tradition of the Jewish community. In his posthumously published *Faith on Earth*, my teacher H. Richard Niebuhr writes: "Theology is an effort to understand a faith that has been given, not an effort to understand in order that we may believe." And again: "We do not first trust in this church and then in God; the relations are direct but double. We trust in God as we have been led to understand the mysterious One by the church.[6]

Dr. Niebuhr continues that Jesus Christ

John Macquarrie, *Principles of Christian Theology*, 2nd ed. (New York: Charles Scribner's Sons, 1977); Thomas C. Oden, *Systematic Theology*, 2 vols. (New York: Harper & Row, 1989); Helmut Thielicke, *Theological Ethics*, 2 vols. (Philadelphia: Fortress Press, 1966, 1969); and Paul Tillich, *Systematic Theology*, 3 vols. (Chicago: University of Chicago Press, 1951, 1957, 1963). See also Edward Farley, *Ecclesial Reflection: An Anatomy of Theological Method* (Philadelphia: Fortress Press, 1982). For a helpful introduction, combining history, theology, and spirituality, consult Sandra S. Frankiel, *Christianity* (San Francisco: Harper & Row, 1985). On a more advanced level of historiography, see Paul Tillich, *A History of Christian Thought: From Its Judaic and Hellenistic Origins to Existentialism*, ed. Carl E. Braaten (New York: Simon and Schuster, 1968).
[4]Ellen T. Chary, review of Rosemary Radford Ruether, *Disputed Questions*, and of Mary Hembrow Snyder, *The Christology of Rosemary Radford Ruether*, in *Journal of Ecumenical Studies* 26 (1989): 743.
[5]Wendy Farley, *Tragic Vision and Divine Compassion* (Louisville: Westminster/John Knox Press, 1990), p. 37.
[6]H. Richard Niebuhr, *Faith on Earth*, ed. Richard R. Niebuhr (New Haven-London: Yale University Press, 1989), pp. 64, 113.

presents himself to us in the whole community of faith in the risen Lord; but without [the] testimony of the Scriptures all our interpretations of who this is we encounter would be confused and full of error. The Word of God, God's address to us, calling us to repentance and to faith in him [comes to us] directly in all the encounters of our life with immovable reality, but how should we understand these words or know who it is who is speaking did we not have the interpreter at our side, the community of faith represented by the Scriptures, speaking to us through them?

. . . . The Scriptures are the indispensable handbook, the indispensable companion, the interpreting community of faith at my side in all my encounters with God, with Christ, with my neighbors.[7]

Niebuhr stops short of affirming that Scripture contains and conveys an actual Word of God for Christians. At this point my position is rather more strongly biblical, being somewhat closer to such interpreters as Karl Barth and Bernhard W. Anderson.[8]

A Conservative – and Conserving – Christian Viewpoint

I shall say a word that brings together the matters of personal commitment, the attested truth of Christian faith, and the purposes of this book.

The study before the reader presents in summary form an interpretation I have come to represent after almost a half century of writing. My work is marked by a quite affirmational, traditional-historical rendering of Christian faith and morality – though not a wholly uncritical one. I speak from the standpoint of the authenticity *(intégrité)* of Christian teaching, and in fairly conservative ways. Entailing as it does a recognition of the uniqueness of the Christian faith and ethic – with special reference to both Christology and the place of the church – my viewpoint will become evident as the book develops. The truth of Christianity stands in its own right, in ways independent of relations or "dialogue" with other peoples or traditions. However, the affirmation of the Christian faith, central to which is the love of neighbor in response to the love of God in Christ, will not impugn other points of view or faiths.

As illustrative of my traditionalist, church-centered Christian outlook, I have often spoken of the Christian faith in and through

---

[7]*Ibid.*, p. 115.
[8]Karl Barth, *The Doctrine of the Word of God*, vol. 1, part 1, trans. G. T. Thomson (Edinburgh: T. and T. Clark, 1936), pp. 156-158, 258, 349; Bernhard W. Anderson, *Rediscovering the Bible* (New York: Association Press, 1951), chap. 1. For a helpful discussion of "The Bible as Revelation," see David Brown, *Invitation to Theology* (Oxford: Basil Blackwell, 1989), pp. 86-89.

its consanguinity with Jewishness and Judaism.[9] I have argued against any ideology – defining that term as subjection to collective self-interest – that would have Christianity supersede *(verdrängen)* Judaism. I agree with Michael McGarry, on the Catholic side, that supersessionism is a form of heresy. At the same time, I have sought with equal force to oppose any reduction of Christian faith to a form of Judaism.

A few commentators have linked me to the persuasion that Christianity is "Judaism for the Gentiles." Such has never been my point of view. That position gets into several difficulties. For one thing, it seems to pass over the essential datum that the original Christian church was Jewish through and through. Are we, ex post facto, to charge that community with being theologically and humanly inauthentic? Further, the interpretation in question unjustifiably turns its back upon the abiding, if relatively small, Jewish-Christian collectivity of today as of earlier centuries. Again, and perhaps most decisive, some of Christianity's teachings are simply not put forward in Judaism, even if it is possible in one or another way to associate them with, or in some instances to derive them from, Judaism. All in all, the allegation I reject is not unparallel to such an inordinate fancy as Judaism is "Christianity for the Jews."

Having said all this, we still have to bear in mind the added truth (today almost a truism) that Jesus of Nazareth is not the received Messiah of the Jewish community as such, simply because he is not held by Jews to meet the criteria of Jewish messianic expectation – though, of course, he is, and must be received as, the Christ of the Christian community.[10] On a prevailing Jewish view,

---

[9]Examples of other recent Christian studies that proceed from or add resources to this point of view include Bernard J. Lee, *The Galilean Jewishness of Jesus: Retrieving the Jewish Origins of Christianity* (New York-Mahwah: Paulist Press, 1988); Peter von der Osten-Sacken, *Christian-Jewish Dialogue: Theological Foundations,* trans. Margaret Kohl (Philadelphia: Fortress Press, 1986); Paul M. van Buren, works listed under note 10 below; and Marvin R. Wilson, *Our Father Abraham: Jewish Roots of the Christian Faith* (Grand Rapids: William B. Eerdmans, 1989). In the matter of Jewish interpretations of Christian faith, see, for example, Fritz A. Rothschild, ed., *Jewish Perspectives on Christianity: Leo Baeck, Martin Buber, Franz Rosenzweig, Will Herberg, and Abraham J. Heschel* (New York: Crossroad, 1990).

[10]Consult Paul M. van Buren, *Discerning the Way: A Theology of the Jewish-Christian Reality* (New York: Seabury Press, 1980); *A Christian Theology of the People Israel,* Part II - *A Theology of the Jewish-Christian Reality* (New York: Seabury Press, 1983); *A Theology of the Jewish-Christian Reality,* Part III - *Christ in Context* (San Francisco: Harper & Row, 1988).

when Messiah comes, the appearance will be accompanied by a great transformation of the world into a realm of peace and justice, something that Jesus of Nazareth neither achieved nor witnessed. (A possibly mediating New Testament passage here, or at least a provocative one, is that of Paul: "No one can say 'Jesus is Lord' except by the Holy Spirit" [I Cor. 12:3].)

A threefold, conservative viewpoint – Christian faith and life as independently authentic, as consanguine with Judaism, yet as nonsupersessionist of Judaism – comprises the foundation of my work in general and of this book in particular, and helps foster whatever individuality this brief study may earn. Another way to express my position is to say that the Christian church stands in a relation to Judaism of both continuity and discontinuity.

Query: If, as is sometimes claimed these days, Judaism is "irredeemably patriarchal,"[11] how can those Christians of today who are disturbed by androcentrism continue to acknowledge Judaism as spiritual mother/father? I do not seek to provide an answer to that question here, other than to remind us that our own Christian heritage has been influenced by androcentrism,[12] not to mention antisemitism.[13]

---

[11] The phrase is taken from Judith Plaskow, *Standing Again at Sinai* (San Francisco: Harper & Row, 1990), p. vii.

[12] Consult, for example, Elisabeth Schüssler Fiorenza, *Claiming the Center: A Feminist Critical Theology of Liberation* (Minneapolis: Winston-Seabury, 1986); *In Memory of Her: A Feminist Theological Reconstruction of Christian Origins* (New York: Crossroad, 1983); Daphne Hampson, *Theology and Feminism* (Oxford: Basil Blackwell, 1990); Elizabeth A Johnson, *She Who Is: The Mystery of God in Feminist Theological Discourse* (New York: Crossroad, 1993); Ann Loades, ed., *Feminist Theology: A Reader* (Louisville: Westminster/John Knox Press, 1990); Joan Wallach Scott, *Gender and the Politics of History* (New York: Columbia University Press, 1988); and Sharon D. Welch, *A Feminist Ethic of Risk* (Minneapolis: Fortress Press, 1990).

[13] Consult, for example, Shmuel Almog, *Antisemitism Through the Ages*, trans. Nathan H. Reisner (Oxford: Pergamon Press, 1988); Joel Carmichael, *The Satanizing of the Jews: Origin and Development of Mystical Anti-Semitism* (New York: Fromm International, 1992); Jeremy Cohen, *The Friars and the Jews: The Evolution of Medieval Anti-Judaism* (Ithaca-London: Cornell University Press, 1982); A. Roy Eckardt, *Your People, My People: The Meeting of Jews and Christians* (New York: Quadrangle/New York Times Book Co., 1974), Part One; John G. Gager, *The Origins of Anti-Semitism: Attitudes Toward Judaism in Pagan and Christian Antiquity* (New York-Oxford: Oxford University Press, 1983); Malcolm Hay, *The Roots of Christian Anti-Semitism* (New York: Freedom Library Press, 1981); William Nicholls, *Christian Antisemitism: A History of Hate* (Northvale, NJ-London: Jason Aronson, 1993); and James Parkes, *Antisemitism* (London: Vallentine, Mitchell, 1963).

Part I

CHRISTIAN TEACHINGS: HUMANKIND AND GOD

2

Who Are These Earthlings?

In this first of our more substantive chapters we grapple with the question of human nature and identity. We do so by reflecting upon the phenomenon of earthlingness.

The Human Being

I once heard a Roman Catholic clergyperson say, "I was a man before I was a priest." Christians are at once human beings and religious believers. People do not cease being human children of the earth when they become Christians, and such people do not cease being Christians because they continue to think and act in human, earthly ways. The two sides are conjoined in the testimony that Christian faith embodies a true humanism *(humanisme intégral).*[1]

To paint the human being as one among many sorts of terrestrials is coherent with the Christian assurance that it is God who makes possible "this world" and all that is therein.[2] From the present point of view, the world is not self-contained or self-perpetuating or accidental, but is instead God's handiwork. Beneath, behind, and beyond the entire realm of nature is God, nature's Ground *(Urgrund).* Therefore, to study humankind and the world of nature is to become involved (stuck?) with questions of religion.

Query: Why is it that the colors of nature do not clash? Again: "Why did the universe start out with so nearly the critical rate of

---

[1]See Jacques Maritain, *Integral Humanism,* trans. Joseph W. Evans (New York: Charles Scribner's Sons, 1968).
[2]I do not imply here (or anywhere) that the existence of God can be finally proved by the human mind. Put more constructively, the God that the human mind may "prove" is not the Jewish or Christian God.

expansion that separates models that recollapse from those that go on expanding forever, so that even now, ten thousand million years later, it is still expanding at the critical rate? If the rate of expansion one second after the big bang had been smaller by even one part in a hundred thousand million million, the universe would have recollapsed before it ever reached its present size."[3] Responding queries: How can it be that so many of the creatures of this world should bring pain and suffering to one another? More particularly, why are so many human males so cruel to females?[4]

To emphasize humankind and humankind's problems as the point of departure for this book rather than choosing the more compelling Christian starting-place of Jesus Christ may seem disordered. I should respond that in the Christian view, Jesus Christ is more an *answer* to the human plight or condition than he is part of the human question as such. We shall later on reckon with the theme of Jesus Christ.

The Glory and the Horror

My understanding of "human being" has been influenced by another teacher of mine, Reinhold Niebuhr, brother of H. Richard. But in attesting as he does to the dialectical (dual) character of humanity as simultaneously a creature of infinite heights and infinite depths, Reinhold Niebuhr is carrying forward and confirming the overall biblical apprehension of humankind.

On the one hand, humanity is seen to be fashioned in the very image of God, is indeed "little lower than God," is crowned "with glory and honor," and has even been given dominion over all "the works" of God's hands (Ps. 8:5-6). On the other hand, humankind is seen to be an incorrigible idol-maker who falls into radical self-deification and in the process subjects itself to self-destructiveness and inflicts its sinfulness upon the rest of creation.[5] Humankind can, singularly, destroy its own kind (not to mention other "kinds") –

---

[3]Stephen Hawking, *A Brief History of Time* (New York: Bantam Books, 1988), pp. 121-122.
[4]According to a study by the Bureau of Justice Statistics of the Justice Department, of the approximately 2.5 million women a year who are robbed, raped, or assaulted in the U.S., about a quarter are victims of family members or men the women have dated. Of the 4 million men a year who are victims of violence, only 6 percent are attacked by family members or females they have dated (*The New York Times*, 20 January 1991).
[5]Consult Reinhold Niebuhr, *The Nature and Destiny of Man,* vol. 1 (New York: Charles Scribner's Sons, 1941); *The Self and the Dramas of History* (New York: Charles Scribner's Sons, 1955).

through war, through exploitation, through oppression, through allied acts of "inhumanity." Upon a Christian view, the human being is a sinner engaged in rebellion against God, but yet a sinner who, because of having been fabricated in the divine image, remains a persisting candidate for righteousness and continues to be eligible for some form of redemption. In this regard, Emil Brunner has entered the provocative judgment that humankind is not great enough to introduce sin into the world. Along the same line, I do not see how we could ever supply an ultimately satisfactory rationale for why humanity should misuse its freedom in order to rebel against God. In earlier centuries the tempting Devil served as a highly qualified "explanation" here, but the Devil has subsequently fallen upon hard times – at least at the point of recognition.[6]

Historic Judaism numbers two impulses within the human spirit: *yetser tov,* an impulse toward goodness, and *yetser ra,* an impulse toward evil. By and large, Christianity has followed along here and affirms the same duality. (But I think a case can be made that, *strictly relative to each other,* and across their histories as a whole, Judaism has stressed somewhat more the *yetser tov* and Christianity has stressed somewhat more the *yetser ra.*) The two viewpoints agree that claims for the exclusive "goodness" or for the exclusive "evil" of humankind are one-sided and hence unconvincing. Humanity is in fact a mixture of good and evil, of altruism and aggression, of kindness and cruelty, of regard for others and of self-centeredness.[7]

---

[6]On the Devil, consult A. Roy Eckardt, *How To Tell God From the Devil: On the Way to Comedy* (forthcoming); Susan R. Garrett, *The Demise of the Devil: Magic and the Demonic in Luke's Writings* (Minneapolis: Fortress Press, 1989); Michael Green, *I Believe in Satan's Downfall* (London: Hodder & Stoughton, 1981); Jeffrey Burton Russell, *The Devil: Perceptions of Evil from Antiquity to Primitive Christianity* (Ithaca: Cornell University Press, 1977); *Lucifer: The Devil in the Middle Ages* (Ithaca: Cornell University Press, 1984); *Mephistopheles: The Devil in the Modern World* (Ithaca: Cornell University Press, 1986); *The Prince of Darkness: Radical Evil and the Power of Good in History* (Ithaca: Cornell University Press, 1988); *Satan: The Early Christian Tradition* (Ithaca: Cornell University Press, 1981); Heiko Oberman, *Luther: Man Between God and the Devil* (New Haven: Yale University Press, 1990); and Frederick Sontag, *The God of Evil: An Argument from the Existence of the Devil* (New York: Harper & Row, 1979).

[7]From a thoroughly humanistic perspective Sidney Hook offers a dialectic of the human condition that remarkably parallels biblical Jewish and Christian anthropology, or perhaps has been made possible by that anthropology: Humanism "sees in us humans something which is at once more wonderful and more terrible than anything else in the universe: the power to make ourselves and the world around us better or worse" (*Out of Step: An Unquiet Life in the 20th Century* [New York: Harper & Row, 1987], p. ix).

Here is how Reinhold Niebuhr explicates human creativity and human sinfulness, as I have elsewhere summarized his view (not without awareness of the partially sexist wording[8]). Niebuhr was in turn influenced by Søren Kierkegaard.

> Niebuhr traces the chronic state of sin to a general predisposition deep within the human spirit as such. With Martin Heidegger, he focuses upon *anxiety* as at once the condition of human achievement and the precondition of sin – the former because anxiety is both the prerequisite and the inspiration of creative acts, the latter because of the accompanying temptation to make idols out of the very same attainments and to gather the universe unto ourselves instead of trusting in God as redeemer. Idolatry is the primal sin. In the Niebuhr view the root of sin, as Ronald H. Stone explains, is "unbelief or lack of trust. Given unbelief, man's anxiety drives him either to claim unconditioned significance for himself or to try to escape the possibilities of freedom by immersing himself in some natural vitality." The human will-to-power, which Niebuhr calls "sin in its quintessential form," does not have some specific, ephemeral cause that is eliminatable; it is instead a generalized, perennial expression of the pathetic attempt to banish the basic insecurity of existence . . . . Niebuhr readily concedes that it is paradoxical to avow "both the inevitability of sin in man's freedom and his responsibility," yet the paradox is to be retained once we bear in mind that alternative views are unable to account for actual human behavior in personal, social, and political life. The depth of the paradox of the human will penetrates as well to the will-to-powerlessness, or the retreat into moral irresponsibility, yet also to the demonic practice of hiding self-regard behind a mask of self-righteousness and a cloak of virtue.[9]

Let us develop a little further the human dialectical condition.

These days some youngsters shoot other youngsters to death, while some youngsters treat their peers with respect. Some parents

---

[8]When speaking anthropologically, Reinhold Niebuhr unexceptionally resorted (writing several decades ago) to "man," "he," "him," etc. Yet since so much of Niebuhr's assessment of "man's" behavior and motives is adversely critical, his usage often has the curious psychological effect of sounding anything but sexist.

[9]A. Roy Eckardt, *For Righteousness' Sake* (Bloomington: Indiana University Press, 1987), p. 169 (slightly reworded). The sources utilized here include Niebuhr, *Nature and Destiny of Man,* vol. 1, pp. 183, 192; Ronald H. Stone, *Reinhold Niebuhr: Prophet to Politicians* (Nashville: Abingdon Press, 1972), pp. 101-102, 97-98; and Gabriel Fackre, *The Promise of Reinhold Niebuhr* (Philadelphia: Lippincott, 1970), pp. 39, 40. In the matter of Søren Kierkegaard's influence upon Niebuhr, see especially Kierkegaard's *The Concept of Anxiety* (Princeton: Princeton University Press, 1980). Upon Reinhold Niebuhr's theological/ethical position as a whole, consult Kenneth Durkin, *Reinhold Niebuhr* (London: Geoffrey Chapman, 1989).

abuse their children, some parents do not. Some husbands batter their wives, some husbands do not. Some people (most usually males) are thieves and/or burglars, some people are not. Some persons are responsibly political-minded, some persons are not. Some people enjoy sports, some people do not.[10] Some people are religious, some people are not. Some people believe in nothing, some people believe in something. Some people tend to tell lies, some tend to tell the truth, some (most?) tend both to lie and tell the truth. Some nations act to conquer other nations, some nations do not.

The operative word in these and all other such cases is *some.* The word "all" simply cannot be used here (with the one lingering – or malignant – exception: all people and nations will die). For humankind is an indeterminate creature. It can do and does do an infinity of differing and even contradictory things. Humankind can rise to pinnacles of creativity and goodness, and fall to abysses of meaninglessness and evil. There is no way to predict which path any given human being or any given society will finally follow. The future has a way of being open (as far as we can tell[11]).

For all its technical and technological hegemony over the rest of nature, humanity remains a creature of nature that one day dies, if not within a life-span of threescore years, then within a hundred years, or, tomorrow, a hundred and fifty years. In the presence of this severe limitation of finitude, human beings give evidence, on balance, of being more determined *by* "the world" than determinative *of* "the world." Time – the temporal flux – has the last say concerning humankind.

Yet this limitation comprises only one side of the story, if a formidable one. As nature evolves, with the consequence that humankind comes along and spreads itself over the cosmic stage, the

---

[10] There are those who look down their noses at the devoted "sports fan." I am sometimes bothered by this. The truth may be that this is all the poor soul finds it possible to venerate or to offer him a modicum of "meaning." Through loyalty to, and participation in, the marvelous exploits of "his team," he somehow becomes a larger self than life would otherwise allow for him. Cf. Michael Novak, *The Joy of Sports* (Lanham, Md.: University Press of America, 1988).

[11] Arguably, "determinism" gains validity in re: the *past,* if only in the sense that no alternative patterns or events remain possible, whereas "indeterminism" gains validity in re: the *future,* if only in the sense that alternative patterns or events seem to remain possible. Cf. S. Paul Schilling: "For increasing numbers of scientists, the traditional notion of a tightly-knit universe with no loose ends is no longer tenable" ("Chance and Order in Science and Theology," *Theology Today* 47 [1991]: 368). Consult also Arthur R. Peacocke, *Creation and the World of Science* (Oxford: Clarendon Press, 1979).

potentialities of the drama itself are transformed, though always within limits. A new kind of actor joins the cast of creatures. Here is an animal that ingests and excretes like any animal but then applies symbolic language to the understanding of its ingestive and excretory functions. Here is a being that creates the *Mona Lisa* but then, with great daring (or foolishness?) subjects even that creation to critical assessment. To be a human is to drive oneself out of the realm of mere quantity, to be *resolute* about things, to have "the courage to be,"[12] to respond to the challenge of living amidst a continuing conversation between quantity and quality.

Human Transcendence

In the language of Reinhold Niebuhr and others, a key concept in the identification of humankind or the human self in its personal and societal dimensions alike is *transcendence,* the faculty of humanity as standing in certain respects "beyond" itself and its world. Humankind is *not* a duality of the "spiritual" and the "material" but rather persists as a single transcending reality, "a creature who thinks and runs, grieves and cries, is amused and laughs."[13] Transcendence involves radical freedom, indeterminate freedom, free self-determination.

A rudimentary analogy may be useful. Suppose that everything in existence were exactly the same shade of a particular color (red, green, whatever). The very fact that one can *imagine* such a state of affairs already shows that the quality of transcendence is making itself known. But the point of the analogy lies in its developing the practical implications of the human ability to imagine things. For if we assume – quite an assumption – that there could be human beings under the rather whimsical state of affairs here fancied, how would a given individual ever be able to state what her or his color was or, for that matter, that they possessed any color at all? In the same way, were humanity *no more than* a being qualitatively indistinguishable from the rest of nature, how could humankind even broach the matter of its difference or lack of difference from nature? It is the very *raising of the question* that helps authenticate the difference, the solitariness, the aloneness, the uniqueness of humanity. (The concept "transcendence" is unavoidably paradoxical

---

[12] Paul Tillich, *The Courage To Be* (New Haven: Yale University Press, 1952).
[13] Michael Wyschogrod, *The Body of Faith* (San Francisco: Harper & Row, 1989), p. 66.

because the word points to the human capability that makes any and all concepts possible.[14])

There is a sense in which humanity transcends not merely the rest of nature but – paradoxically – humanity as well. This is seen not only in the human's possession of a self-image as, from one point of view, an object in and of nature. It is seen more positively in the restless human urge toward the fulfillment of as yet absent potentialities. This urge is linked to the wonder of awareness and, more astonishingly, to our being aware that the wonder of awareness is something wonderful. The urge incarnates itself in humankind's engagement of itself in an ongoing internal dialogue. The human self continually precedes itself. And it constantly runs ahead of itself by fashioning its own aspirations. All this produces a momentous tension among the three temporal dimensions of the past, actual present, and ideal future – among what "has been," "is," and "ought to be."

"Transcendence" is anything but a purely intellectualist faculty. Rather it is an *existential* quality in that it reaches out to and enshrines all aspects of the human reality. Accordingly, any effort to "prove" that there is such a thing as transcendence or to subject it to various confirmation tests is redundant and may simply lead to embarrassment all around. For transcendence precedes and is presupposed in any process of verification – in the possibility of engaging in proof and in the possibility of searching for truth – just as self-determination is presupposed within the psyche of both the person who argues for "freedom of the will" and the person who argues against free will. No determinist would consent to any insinuation that it is not *they* who are defending determinism. In like manner, should someone see fit to deny that they are a self-transcending being, they will have already presumed transcendence in and through the act of denial. Were this not the case, denial would not be genuine but merely a clatter of sounds. To say no, to say maybe, to say yes, to refuse to say anything – these alternatives give content to the life of transcendence. The eggs of self-denial, self-neglect, self-doubt, self-attention, self-affirmation, self-confidence, and any other conceivable "self-" idea all lie side-by-side within the womb of transcendence. Transcendence is the concretion of human potentiality, the unlimited possibility of seeking to attain unto as

---

[14] Of course, "nature" itself can be readily defined in a way broad enough to encompass the self- and world-transcending being known as humankind. This does not compromise our point. On such a broad definition we should simply agree that humanity is to be identified as that aspect or dimension of nature which acts in certain ways to transcend itself and its world.

yet unfulfilled moral and spiritual possibilities. As David Birnbaum writes, humankind is "an explorer expedition – with its own scouts way up in their cold, wet, and lonely crow's nests. Sweeping the skyline end to end with their lucky eyepieces. Scanning for new land mass. Ah, there! peeking over the horizon! There it is! – or was it only a midshipman's mirage?"[15]

How many times people lament: "If only I could find the word that says what I want to say!" Here is manifest the inner bond between transcendence and language. To be transcendent, to act transcendingly, is to be in anguish or at least discomfort over the "right word" – more especially, it seems, as humans grow older. They seek to clarify their terminologies as much as possible, in order to bridge creatively and responsibly the gap between conceptual activity and the requirements of a discriminating human life and daily experience. Perhaps what should worry them is not so much their verbal inadequacies – these can always be worked on – but the dead time when they may cease to be dissatisfied with the words they throw out across the gap.

Thrownness

To dwell upon humankind as part of the natural world (yet at the same time as acting to transcend that world) is implicitly to point up a highly enigmatic, awesome, even potentially terrifying fact.

To be a human being is to be thrust out into reality entirely apart from having any say in the matter. In *Pirke Aboth* we are reminded: "not of thy will wast thou formed."[16] It could be interjected that any alternative state of affairs would be utterly fantastic. Yet this does not make any less strange the truth that the autonomy human beings ostensibly possess is the autonomy of creatures who, at the all-decisive point of their very own origin and ground, are anything but autonomous.

The truth that no one ever asks to be born sets the stage, I suggest, for the entire problem and pathos of being and remaining human (as of being and remaining anything else). It shows in an all-too-evident way that the final responsibility for human existence is carried by some one or something (some thing) other than human beings themselves. This makes it impossible to hold humankind

---

[15]David Birnbaum, *God and Evil* (Hoboken: Ktav Publishing House, 1989), p. 82.
[16]*Pirke Aboth: The Ethics of the Talmud,* ed. R. Travers Herford (New York: Schocken Books, 1978), p. 123 (IV.29).

responsible, *in any ultimate sense,* for what it does with its life. (The question of the legitimacy of suicide here opens up. For Albert Camus, "there is but one major philosophical problem and that is whether or not to commit suicide."[17] True, *Pirke Aboth* continues, "not of thy will dost thou die," but I do not see that this resolves the issue of self-destruction, simply because the world-be suicide can quite licitly protest, "It is God's will that I die this way."[18])

I wrote above "in any ultimate sense," since in no way do I question human responsibility – which often encompasses culpability – for human actions at less than ultimate levels.

The "self-made man" remains a consummate falsehood, a consummate cheat, a consummate joke.

While the recognition that humankind is subject for its entire existence to a power or powers other than itself cannot but condition one's understanding of humanity (as of the world in its entirety), it also makes possible the Christian faith, together with all other faiths. On the one hand, here is a basis for contending that, looked at from *within,* humankind is in a fundamental way alien to its own world – unlike this blissfully unknowing tree, that blissfully ignorant bird, this blissfully unknowing sister leopard, that blissfully ignorant brother horse.[19] Yet, on the other hand, ways are available that help humans to be and to become at home within the great world. For example, in the tractate *Sanhedrin* (37b) it is said: A "reason why God created a single human being was to proclaim the greatness of the Holy One, blessed be He. Man stamps many coins with a single die and they are all identical, but the King of Kings, the Holy One, blessed be He, stamped every man with the seal of the primal man yet no one of them is like his neighbor. Therefore each man may say

---

[17] Albert Camus, *The Myth of Sisyphrus,* trans. Justin O'Brien (New York: Alfred A. Knopf, 1955), p. 3.

[18] Upon suicide as a moral issue, consult John B. Cobb, Jr., *Matters of Life and Death* (Louisville: Westminster/John Knox Press, 1991), chap. 2, "The Right to Die." Cobb deals primarily, not with suicide as such, but with "the right to terminate one's own life when it has become permanently meaningless and painful." For Cobb, "right" is "a shorthand way of describing duties owed to an individual by all other people, duties that are derivative from the nature of that individual" (pp. 10, 16). See also James T. Clemons, ed., *Perspectives on Suicide* (Louisville: Westminster/John Knox Press, 1990); and Clemons, *What Does the Bible Say About Suicide?* (Minneapolis: Fortress Press, 1990).

[19] A further significant contrast is that humans are the ones who give names to the other creatures. It is sad that those creatures can never really appropriate or enjoy their names in the way that humans do.

'for my sake was the world created'"[20] – not excepting that individual who is sobered and even abashed by an awareness that the spiral-armed galaxy scientists have called NGC 1232 is approximately 65 million light years away from Planet Earth. Quality and quantity live, it is true, as sisters within one and the same universe, yet they must never be confused with one another.[21]

In Summary

To bring together what has been no more than a slender review of the human condition: The human being or earthling is at once (a) a finite, wholly dependent organism (an animal amongst the animals) and (b) a cultural-historical being (at once determined by "the world" yet self-determining), who (c) lives within one or another socio-cultural matrix but who (d) both judges or evaluates herself/himself and the matrix as well, and also – "divinely" yet often demonically – reshapes that matrix to various extents through her/his own thinking and behavior. Human *freedom* entails an inner and responsible acceptance of this world together with the energy and the labor to initiate action within the limits of possibility and to transform (constructively and/or destructively) specific states of affairs. Human uniqueness is seen in the fact that humankind *makes* history in unprecedented and fresh ways at the same time that humankind is being *made by* history.

---

[20] As quoted in Morris Adler, *The World of the Talmud*, 2nd ed. (New York: Schocken Books, 1963), p. 69.
[21] Consult Ernst Bloch, *Natural Law and Human Dignity* (Cambridge: MIT Press, 1986); Arthur Peacocke, *Creation and the World of Science; Theology For a Scientific Age* (Cambridge: Basil Blackwell, 1991); and John F. Haught, *The Cosmic Adventure: Science, Religion, and the Quest for Purpose* (New York: Paulist Press, 1984).

3

Who Are These Christian Earthlings?

The Christian faith is affirmed from within a number of options that vie for acceptance, rejection, or non-attention, under the aegis of the self-transcending faculty of humankind.

The Image of God

It is a striking fact of our vast universe that living relations should come to be built between human earthlings and God or the gods. How does this come about? I say "striking fact" not because claims of a divine-human link are rare – they are anything but rare in human history – but simply because "human" and "divine" are, after all, quite disparate aspects of reality.

In the biblical view there is a special instrumentality through which God can relate to humanity, and humanity can relate to God: the *imago dei*, the human being made after the very image of God (*betzelem Elohim*) (Gen. 1:26-27). The teaching of the *imago dei* is the religious counterpart or reflection of the human faculty of transcendence or freedom as we have just been reflecting upon it. God is Godself a transcending or free being, and, accordingly, the two realities, divine and human, are able to meet:

Seek the Lord while he may be found,
    call upon him while he is near;
let the wicked forsake their way,
    and the unrighteous their thoughts;
let them return to the Lord, that
    he may have mercy on them,
and to our God, for he will

abundantly pardon.
For my thoughts are not your thoughts,
　　nor are your ways my ways, says the Lord.
For as the heavens are higher than the earth,
　　so are my ways higher than your ways
　　and my thoughts than your thoughts
　　　　　　　　　　　　　(Isa. 55:6-9).

It is in and through the image of God that the door is opened to the discrete Christian hope and claim of membership within God's people.

Manifold Peoples of God

Testimony within Scripture declares that there are, and are to be, many peoples of God.

Did I not bring Israel up from
　　the land of Egypt,
and the Philistines from
　　Caphtor and the
　　Arameans from Kir?
　　　　　　　　　　　　(Amos 9:7).

Thus says the Lord to his
　　anointed, to Cyrus [the Persian],
whose right hand I have
　　grasped
to subdue nations before him
　　and strip kings of their robes, . . . :
I will go before you
　　and level the mountains, . . .
so that you may know that it is
　　I, the Lord,
the God of Israel, who call you
　　by your name
　　　　　　　　　　　　(Isa. 45:1-3).

"Lord, who will not fear
　　and glorify your name?
For you alone are holy.
　　All nations will come
　　and worship before you,

for your judgments have been
revealed"

(Rev. 15:4; cf. Jer. 10:7; Ps. 86:9-10).[1]

Israel as the People of God

However, within the aggregation "peoples of God," Israel is singled out as a particular or special people of God. Indeed, for Scripture the God of creation and the nations is, or is gradually seen to be, always identical with the God of Israel.

> Now the Lord said to Abram, "Go from your country and your kindred and your father's house [in Ur of the Chaldeans] to the land that I will show you. I will make of you a great nation, and I will bless you, and make your name great, so that you will be a blessing
> . . . ."
>
> "As for me, this is my covenant with you: . . . . No longer shall your name be Abram, but your name shall be Abraham; for I have made you the ancestor of a multitude of nations. . . . I will establish my covenant between me and you, and your offspring after you throughout their generations for an everlasting covenant, to be God to you and to your offspring after you . . ."
>
> (Gen. 12:1-2; 17:4-5, 7).

Traditionally, we speak of "the God of Abraham, Isaac, and Jacob." With the strange event at the ford of the Jabbok, where "a man wrestled with him [Jacob] until daybreak," Jacob's name became Israel. He "called the place Peniel, saying, 'For I have seen God face to face, and yet my life is preserved'" (Gen. 32: 24-30). Thus was first denominated the "God of Israel" in the exact sense – the same One who generations later is to assure Moses:

> Now therefore, if you obey my voice and keep my covenant, you shall be my treasured possession out of all the peoples. Indeed, the whole earth is mine, but you shall be for me a priestly kingdom and a holy nation (Ex. 19:5 6).

It is in response to God's grace-full choice of Israel that Israel chooses God to be its God.

> And Joshua said to all the people. . . . "Now therefore fear the Lord, and serve him in sincerity and in faithfulness. . . . Now if you are unwilling to serve the Lord, choose this day whom you will serve, whether the gods your ancestors served in the region beyond the River or the gods of the Amorites in whose land you are living;

---

[1] According to Genesis, after the Flood God also covenants with "every living creature, . . . the birds, the domestic animals, and every animal of the earth" (Gen. 9:10).

but as for me and my household, we will serve the Lord" (Josh. 24:2, 14-15).

For its part, Israel looked and looks upon itself as in some way set apart from the "nations" (as does the Christian community, and as do other "chosen" peoples). Such self-concentration is often counteracted and refined by the objective command of "service" to the Lord. What it means to "serve the Lord" will occupy us – and perplex us – in later pages. For the present, two comments of Michael Wyschogrod are apropos. First, "by electing the seed of Abraham, God creates a people that is in his service in the totality of its human being and not just in its moral and spiritual existence." I should argue in an identical way respecting the Christian church – though not having ignored Judith Plaskow's stricture: Wyschogrod also "talks about circumcision as a sign of the covenant as if Jewish women do not exist."[2] Second, there is the importance that attaches to the nation within the teaching of the covenant.

> To believe that the individual can be lifted out of his nation and brought into relation with God is as illusory as to believe that man's soul can be saved and his body discarded. Just as man is body and soul, so man is an individual and member of a nation. To save him as an individual and to leave the national social order unredeemed is to truncate man and then to believe that this remnant of a human being is the object of salvation. The national election of Israel is therefore . . . a sign of God's understanding of the human predicament and the confirmation of and love for that humanity. By sanctifying the nationhood of Israel, God confirms the national order of all peoples and expresses his love for the individual in his national setting and for the nations in their corporate personalities.[3]

The Church as the People of God

With the event of Jesus Christ, a certain Jewish woodworker from Nazareth, the Christian church is granted, or comes to maintain,

---

[2]Judith Plaskow, *Standing Again at Sinai* (San Francisco: Harper & Row, 1990), p. 243. The reference in Michael Wyschogrod is *The Body of Faith* (San Francisco: Harper & Row, 1987), p. 67.
[3]Wyschogrod, *Body of Faith,* pp. 67, 68. The unfortunately sexist (i.e., androcentric) language of these passages will be noted. But to keep pointing up such all-too prevalent practice within the sources I cite would be tedious; let my adverse comment here suffice regarding additional cititations of that kind in succeeding pages.
For a Christian presentation of the divine covenant with Israel, consult Paul M. van Buren, *A Christian Theology of the People Israel,* Part II, *A Theology of the Jewish-Christian Reality* (New York: Seabury Press, 1983).

separate identification, although only by being conjoined to Israel as the people of God:

> So then, remember that at one time you Gentiles by birth . . . —
> remember that you were at that time without Christ, being aliens
> from the commonwealth of Israel, and strangers to the covenants of
> promise, having no hope and without God in the world. But now in
> Christ Jesus you who once were far off have been brought near by the
> blood of Christ. . . So then you are no longer strangers and aliens, but
> you are citizens with the saints and also members of the household
> of God . . . (Eph. 2:11-13, 19).

This does not mean that God has spurned or turned away from God's people Israel. No, for as Paul writes, "God has not rejected his people whom he foreknew. . . . The gifts and the call of God are irrevocable." Indeed, Israel remains the root that supports the church. The Christian community has been added on to Israel, "grafted into" Israel, as a new reality within the comprehensive people/s of God: "O the depth of the riches and wisdom and knowledge of God! How unsearchable are his judgments and how inscrutable his ways! (Rom. 11:2, 29, 18, 24, 33). The opening of God's covenant to those beyond Israel helps to implement the promise, repeated a number of times in Genesis (12:3; 18:18; 22:18; 26:4; 28:14), that Abraham and Abraham's posterity will be a source of blessing to all the peoples of the world.[4]

Christians are a people, not in the strict meaning of a nation or race or ethnic group, but in the sense of a community of faith. In this they at once take after and diverge from their spiritual mothers and fathers, the Jewish people. Judaism is of course a religious faith, and Jewishness obviously encompasses a community of faith, but in addition Jewishness extends to a people *(laos)* in more than a discretely or narrowly religious understanding. Jewish existence is tied to "the destiny of a national family," a "natural family."[5] It entails what Rabbi Abraham Isaac calls "normal holiness." By contrast, there is great doubt that Christianness or Christian integrity could ever be sustained apart from its specifically religious substance.

Let us sharpen the difference here. Peter von der Osten-Sacken speaks of "Israel's presence in the church: the Jewish-Christians."[6] As we have already noted, there are Christians in the church today

---

[4]A. Roy Eckardt, *For Righteousness' Sake* (Bloomington: Indiana University Press, 1987), p. 270.
[5]Wyschogrod, *Body of Faith,* pp. xvii, xv.
[6]Peter von der Osten-Sacken, *Christian-Jewish Dialogue,* trans. Margaret Kohl (Philadelphia: Fortress Press, 1986), chapter 4.

of Jewish laic background, and many of these people (they are not a large group) insist that to be a Christian is to be no less a Jew.[7] But now turn the language around: "the church's presence in Israel: the Christian-Jews." Such a construction is not tenable, in contrast to the other one. For what could it mean to claim that a Christian who becomes a Jew is or could still be a Christian?

The central truth abides nonetheless that the Christian community of faith receives its meaning from its foundation in Israel. The Israel of Hebrew Scripture (the Tanak) is called to be people of God, and the Christian community follows in a like train. Indeed, the very uniqueness of Christianity derives from the church's grounding in the sacred history of Israel. As Karl Barth has said, Christians are mere guests in the house of Israel.[8]

Thus it is that the Christian faith stands in essential continuity with Judaism with respect to *people of God*, and at the same time stands in some discontinuity with Judaism and Jewishness in that within Christianity "people of God" becomes a specifically or delimitedly religious kind of persuasion. Of course, as we will emphasize, the religious quality of the Christian gospel has great bearing upon human life and the world as a whole; no final separation is allowable between "spiritual" and "material," "sacred" and "profane." The present point is simply that while Jewishness is at one and the same time a religious and an extrareligious category – many Jews can be quite "irreligious" yet still be Jews – it is as a religious or spiritual category that Christianness as such is able to live.[9]

Many persons and groups think of themselves as chosen by God or by some divine being. I can find no convincing reason, in principle, to adjudge that they are wrong (see especially chapter 7, section titled Sister/Brother Faiths). It is entirely possible to affirm one's own spiritual chosenness without excluding or denigrating the chosenness of others. And yet, any self- or group-affirmation of a divine choice or election remains ever open to the danger of individual and collective arrogance and idolatry. How tempting it is to forget the warning given voice by the prophet Amos:

---

[7]These Christians are represented in the International Messianic Jewish (Hebrew Christian) Alliance.

[8]A. Roy Eckardt, *Elder and Younger Brothers* (New York: Charles Scribner's Sons, 1967; Schocken Books, 1973), pp. 51, 158.

[9]I sometimes wonder whether there may be a special vocation for some people to remain at one and the same time on the border of the church and on the border of the synagogue, perhaps in that way witnessing to a bond between the two sides.

You only have I known
     of all the families of the earth;
therefore I will punish you
     for all your iniquities
                                        (Amos 3:2).

To be chosen of God is to be granted peculiar opportunities for blessedness – but also to be held to peculiar obligations. Indeed, there is no blessedness without obligation. But does not this apply to God as much as it does to humankind?:

Far be it from you . . . to slay the righteous with the wicked . . . .
Far be that from you! Shall not the Judge of all the earth do what
is just? (Gen. 18:25).

Once the perplexing question of the divine-human relationship comes to engage us, additional questions arise respecting the flawed character of that relationship. This takes us over into chapter four.

4

God: From Void to Enemy to Friend?

It is said that Scripture proffers a life story of God.

Blame Vis-à-Vis Accountability

The teaching that God "punishes" or may "punish" human beings, not excluding God's own people, is found in some religions. Presupposed here is human blameworthiness for sin; how else could this kind of divine behavior be considered moral? Of equal or greater import is the threat such "punishment" may bring to the teaching of the divine goodness and integrity, and this upon several grounds. For one thing, we have already commented upon the shattering truism of no human say in the originating presence of humankind in this world. How could it be morally licit to punish without qualification a humanity that has had, as integral persons, no voice in its one and only created life? Second, there is the issue of how to reconcile God's wrath to God's love. Third, and behind every other question, we face the enigma of whether God is hostile or friendly to humankind or, arguably, whether God may be both of these at once.

Again, how could it be that the reputed Sovereign of the world would permit the murder of six millions of the children of Israel in the *Shoah* (Holocaust), "a perfected figuration of the demonic" (Arthur A. Cohen)?[1] Or the slaughter of (what was eventually to become) some 400,000 Japanese at Hiroshima and Nagasaki?[2] Or the

---

[1]Arthur A. Cohen, *The Tremendum* (New York: Crossroad, 1981), p. 48.

[2]An estimated 115,000 to 135,000 Japanese were killed immediately, and a great many more were burned, maimed, and otherwise injured. After one year the deaths had reached 210,000. Forty years afterward bomb-related injuries and diseases accounted for some 315,000-340,000 deaths, and any final count is

killing of up to 200,000 Iraqis (mostly by "Coalition," and particularly American, forces) in the U.N.-Iraq War of 1991?

Martin Buber wrote: "One can still 'believe' in a God who allowed [such] things to happen, but how can one still speak to Him?"[3] Numbers alone are not the crucial consideration; the suffering and death of one little child is sufficient to press the question of God's goodness/power. Dostoevsky's Ivan Karamazov protests: "There is no justification for the tear of a single suffering child." And yet, as David Birnbaum points out, it is the death of millions that "unnerves the mass of humanity" and "opens the gates for a communal introspection and theological reassessment."[4]

Nor does it help to limit final moral blame to human beings for great annihilations of human lives. In barely sixteen words Eliezer Berkovits bars that way out: "God is responsible for having created a world in which man is free to make history."[5]

The searing question of the enmity/friendliness of God is given concerted attention in the work of H. Richard Niebuhr, whose influence is reflected, though not uncritically, in the present chapter.

Niebuhr inquires how the question of God presents itself to those who stand within the living tradition of Protestant Christianity: "It comes to us as an eminently practical problem, a problem of human existence and destiny, of the meaning of human life in general and of the life of the self and its community in particular. It does not arise for us in the speculative form of such questions as 'Does God exist?' or 'What is the first cause, what the ultimate substance?' Our first question is *'How is faith in God possible?'*"[6]

---

still incomplete (Alice L. Eckardt and A. Roy Eckardt, *Long Night's Journey Into Day: A Revised Retrospective on the Holocaust* [Detroit: Wayne State University Press; Oxford: Pergamon Press, 1988], pp. 62-63).

[3]Martin Buber lecture, "The Dialogue Between Heaven and Earth," cited in Emil L. Fackenheim, *To Mend the World* (New York: Schocken Books, 1989), p. 196. Consult also Elie Wiesel and Philippe-Michaël de Saint Cheron, *Evil and Exile*, trans. Jon Rothschild (Notre Dame-London: University of Notre Dame Press, 1990).

[4]David Birnbaum, *God and Evil* (Hoboken: Ktav Publishing House, 1989), pp. 4, 7. Such horrific events as the Holocaust, Hiroshima, and Nagasaki are absolutely unique, i.e., unprecedented. Yet the murder of innocents is an age-old phenomenon. Individual suffering is always unique.

[5]Eliezer Berkovits, "The Hiding God of History," in Yisrael Gutman and Livia Rothkirchen, eds., *The Catastrophe of European Jewry: Antecedents-History-Reflections* (Jerusalem: Yad Vashem, 1976), p. 704.

[6]H. Richard Niebuhr, *Radical Monotheism and Western Culture* (New York: Harper and Brothers, 1960), pp. 115-116.

Faith as Unavoidable

"To be a self is to be the kind of being which can and must bind itself by promises to other selves; which must keep faith with others; which in this I-Thou relationship of loyal-disloyal promise makers trusts and distrusts."[7]

Although it is so that only limited numbers of persons are fervent in their loyalty to one or another historic religion, it is difficult if not impossible for human beings to escape having some kind of faith – faith in the dimension of a "practical trusting in, reliance on, counting upon something . . . . that has power or is power," a committing of the human self to what H. Richard Niebuhr speaks of as a "center of value" (or what Paul Tillich denominates our "ultimate concern"). Says Niebuhr: "Not only the just but also the unjust, insofar as they live, live by faith." Again, "there is no escape from life in faith and no escape from an existence in which all trust and faithfulness is malformed by distrust and treason."[8] In here presenting a phenomenology of human faith, Niebuhr is not necessarily implying that faith is inherently "good," or that unfaith is inherently "bad."

Then there is the specific form of faith or confidence that "may above all else be called religious, because it is related to our existence as worshiping beings, even as our faith in the intelligibility of nature is related to our existence as knowing beings and our confidence in each other is related to our moral life. This is the faith that life is worth living, or better, the reliance on certain centers of value as able to bestow significance and worth on our existence . . . . [For] we cannot live without a cause, without some

---

[7]H. Richard Niebuhr, *Faith on Earth* (New Haven-London: Yale University Press, 1989), p. 63. This study by Niebuhr offers an intensive phenomenology of the nature of faith. John P. Boyle identifies the "phenomenology of religion" as engaging in "a careful description of religious manifestations of all sorts with the aim of allowing the nature or essence of religion to appear" ("Paradigms for Public Education Religion Studies Curricula: Some Suggestions and Critique," *The Council on the Study of Religion Bulletin* 12 [1981]: 41). Always at issue, of course, is whether such procedures can nurture *understanding;* also whether phenomena can ever convey something about noumena. The second of these is the more problematic question and even a heartrending one.

[8]Niebuhr, "The Center of Value," *Radical Monotheism*, pp. 100-113; D. Mackenzie Brown, *Ultimate Concern. Tillich in Dialogue* (New York: Harper Colophon Books, 1965); Niebuhr, *Radical Monotheism*, pp. 116-118; *Faith on Earth*, p. 85.

object of devotion, some center of worth, something on which we rely for our meaning."[9]

The Gods at War,
The Twilight of the Gods

Having construed the word and indeed the reality "god" as "the object of human faith in life's worthwhileness," H. Richard Niebuhr enters upon what may be dubbed the war amongst the gods. Such strife is made real in and through the truth that the faith by which humans live tends to be "a multifarious thing with many objects of devotion and worship." These include one's own self, most common of all objects of devotion; one's sons and daughters; one's home; sex; and the various "Olympian gods – our country, our ideologies, our democracies, civilizations, churches, our art which we practice for art's sake, our truth which we pursue for truth's sake, our moral values, our ideas and the social forces which we personalize, adore, and on which we depend for deliverance from sheer nothingness and the utter inconsequence of existence."[10]

Yet there remains a horror: the twilight of the gods.

> None of these beings on which we rely to give content and meaning to our lives is able to supply continuous meaning and value. The causes for which we live all die. The great social movements pass and are supplanted by others. The ideals we fashion are revealed by time to be relative. The empires and cities to which we are devoted all decay. At the end nothing is left to defend us against the void of meaninglessness. We try to evade this knowledge, but it is ever in the background of our minds. The apocalyptic vision of the end of all things assails us, whether we see that end as the prophets of the pre-Christian era did or as the pessimists of our time do. We know that "on us and all our race the slow, sure doom falls pitiless and dark" [Bertrand Russell]. All our causes, all our ideas, all the beings on which we relied to save us from worthlessness are doomed to pass.[11]

But, you and I may respond, why does not such a fate afflict as well the God of Israel and of Jesus Christ?

Metanoia *in Heaven*

H. Richard Niebuhr's move from the gods who can only fail to the God who does not fail, indeed from God as Void to God as Enemy to God as Friend, is made possible by the question: What is it that is

---

[9]Niebuhr, *Radical Monotheism*, p. 118.
[10]*Ibid.*, pp. 119-120.
[11]*Ibid.*, pp. 121-122.

responsible for the transitoriness and the doom of the many human gods? I should incline to answer – at least prefatorily yet in accord with an emphasis of chapter two – by taking notice of the Whatever that has thrust humanity into life with no consent of humans, the Whatever that in an astonishing yet objective way is glimpsed as counterpart to the same secrecy, mystery, and alienness that pursue the inner lives, fortunes, and destinies of human beings. Niebuhr replies in allied terms:

> We may call it the nature of things, we may call it fate, we may call it reality. But by whatever name we call it, this law of things, this reality, this way things are, is something with which we must reckon. We may not be able to give a name to it, calling it only the "void" out of which everything comes and to which everything returns, though that is also a name. But it is there – the last shadowy and vague reality, the secret of existence by virtue of which things come into being, are what they are, and pass away. Against it there is no defense. This reality, this nature of things, abides when all else passes. It is the source of all things and the end of all. It surrounds our life as the great abyss into which all things plunge and as the great source whence they all come. What it is we do not know save that it is and that it is the supreme reality with which we must reckon.

Yet how does it happen that this Void, this Existent against which humans have no defense, may itself become the object of their faith, even of their love? How can it be that this "enemy of all our causes," this "opponent of all our gods," should come to win the confidence of people and gain their devotion, should in fact become the reality they celebrate as none other than God? For such transformation has in truth taken place and continues to take place within human history. To Alfred North Whitehead, authentic religion means "transition from God the void to God the enemy, and from God the enemy to God the companion." The *metanoia* of God, an apodictic turn-around of God, does occur, as reflected in scriptural testimony. There is a psalmist who sings,

> Whom have I in heaven but you?
>> And there is nothing on earth
>>> that I desire other than you
>>>> (Ps. 73:25).

There is a Job who, while protesting,

> Why do you hide you face,
>> and count me as your enemy?
>>> (Job 13:24).

also declares,

> Though he slay me, yet will
>   I trust in him
>
> (Job 13:15, *KJV*).

The transformation happens in divergent ways amongst diverse people. As Niebuhr continues, for Christians it happens through

> the concrete meeting with Jesus Christ . . . . [We] confront in the event of Jesus Christ the presence of that last power which brings to apparent nothingness the life of the most loyal man. Here we confront the slayer, and here we become aware that this slayer is the life-giver. He does not put to shame those who trust in him. In the presence of Jesus Christ we [who are Christians] most often conceive, or are given that faith . . . .
>
> So it is in history. This faith in the One has had its occasional manifestations elsewhere [only "occasional"? – A.R.E.]. But it has happened in history that it has been conceived and received where a people who regarded themselves as chosen suffered the most cruel fate, and where a Son of man who was obedient to death actually suffered death. Here the great reconciliation with the divine enemy has occurred. [12]

The truth abides, the history stands: The One who appears as Enemy also acts to be the humans' Friend; the divine It becomes the divine Thou. Here is the height and the depth of faith, within the biblical witness as a whole. In *Faith on Earth* H. Richard Niebuhr adduces a trinity of *fides, fiducia,* and *fidelitas,* thus providing "three parts of one interpersonal action in which *fides* (believing) is the phenomenal element which is largely based on the fundamental interaction of *fiducia* (trust) and *fidelitas* (loyalty or fidelity)." The trust of faith issues in loyalty, loyalty to the Other in and through the very claim or claims the Other makes. For in consequence of the coming of Jesus Christ "we are able to say in the midst of our vast distrust, our betraying and being betrayed, our certainty of death and our temptations to curse our birth: 'Abba, our Father.' And this we say to the Ground of Being, to the mystery out of which we come, to the power over our life and death. 'Our Father, who art in heaven, hallowed be thy name' (Matt. 6:9-12; Luke 11:2-4). 'I believe, help thou mine unbelief' (Mark 9:24)." [13]

Niebuhr fills out his analysis of "the structure of faith" by allying certain personalist considerations with certain religious considerations, and in terms not narrowly Christian.

---

[12] *Ibid.,* pp. 122-125.
[13] Niebuhr, *Faith on Earth,* pp. 47-48, 59, 96-97.

The reality of selfhood or, to use the good old-fashioned term, of the soul, comes to appearance in the activity of trusting and distrusting, being loyal and deceiving. The reality of an other self is acknowledged, depended upon in the act of trusting and distrusting, being faithful to him and deceiving him. The reality of God, of the Transcendent One, is obscurely acknowledged in life's distrust and anxiety and openly so in trust in Him, loyalty to Him and loyalty to the objects of his loyalty. The certainty of faith may be stated in a somewhat Cartesian fashion: I believe (i.e., trust-distrust, swear allegiance and betray) therefore I know that I am, but also I trust you and therefore I am certain that you are, and I trust and distrust the Ultimate Environment, the Absolute Source of my being, therefore I acknowledge that He is. There are three realities of which I am certain, self, companions and the Transcendent.[14]

The way to and from God (also away from God) is thus not one of philosophic speculation or reflection but of life-and-death decision-making, within the praxis and turmoil of everyday living. And the inevitably accompanying question is whether we who have somehow come to survive until today are going to count ourselves part of, or alternatively to dissociate ourselves from, a previous yet ongoing and shared story, the history of a community of faith that continues to live (the Christian community? the Jewish community? the Muslim community?).

I come at last to my promised critical reaction to Niebuhr. I believe that the very exactitude of his phrasing in *Radical Monotheism* must continue to give serious pause: "the great reconciliation with the divine enemy." I think that we have to receive these words dialectically – which means with great caution – because of an anguishing truth: While it is so that the Enemy becomes the Friend, the human being is still compelled to mourn that the Friend appears to remain as Enemy. To proceed otherwise would be to fall into a Polyanna complex of spiritual complacency, unrealism, and sentimentality. Christians can hardly allow their faith to be blind, nor can they be content with irrational leaps into the dark. The *metanoia* of God from Enemy to Friend simply does not, from an honest and integral human point of view, wholly eradicate God as Enemy (any more than it disposes of God as Void). The question and the promise of the divine *metanoia* are no more than those of the direction God is going and yearns to go, the question of God's own life story. Christian faith entails the trust that God as Friend is overtaking and will in the end overtake God as Enemy. But the Christian identification of God as Friend, however much it is

---

[14]*Ibid.*, p. 61. Cf. chap. 5 of the same work, "Broken Faith."

legitimated by the Christian experience of Jesus Christ, does not eliminate the truth that this One continues to give *some kind of consent* – if God is indeed *the* universal One – to disease and rape, to war and typhoon,[15] to anxiety and hunger, to meaninglessness and despair, to destruction and death. Here is perhaps the most terrible or at least the most humbling spiritual admission the believing Christians must make: that even amidst the great fullness of Christian faith, God abides as Void, even as Enemy. Thus are we compelled to move, not alone from Void to Enemy to Friend, but also from Friend to Enemy to Void. (Yet what religion – or non-religion – can elude this dread qualification?) Jesus himself is left to cry out upon his cross, "My God, my God, why have you forsaken me?" (Matt. 27:46): "God, my Friend, why are you my Enemy?"

A Single Moral Standard

We have not as yet met the most piercing question of all. How are human beings to endure the anguish of affirming a God that is *at once* Enemy/Friend? Is not such an unending dialectical condition – the very ultimate in ambivalence – more than the human spirit can stand or ought to stand?

In tentative response I submit David Birnbaum's reminder that Israel has never yielded its right to ask and to avow "that God's justice be morally justifiable and answerable, as well, to the standard" God has set for humankind. I suggest that as Israel goes, so may go the Christian church. Birnbaum brings home the truth that Scripture encompasses a "protest literature" that opposes all double standards that God expostulates for humanity.[16]

> Why does the way of the guilty
>   prosper?
> Why do all who are
>   treacherous thrive?
>
>   (Jer. 12:1).
>
> Why do you hide your face?
>   Why do you forget our

---

[15] In their phrase "acts of God" insurance companies engage in a curious kind of theology. How could one particular catastrophic act qualify as an "act of God" while another such act becomes a "non-act of God"? Once it is maintained that, ultimately speaking, God is the responsible party in everything that happens, distinctions of this kind are seen as arbitrary.

[16] Birnbaum, *God and Evil*, pp. 48-49. The scriptural passages that follow are among those mustered by Birnbaum.

> affliction and oppression?
>
> (Ps. 44:24).

> Far be it from me to say that you
>   are right;
> until I die I will not put away
>   my integrity from me.
> I hold fast my righteousness, and
>   will not let it go . . .
>
> (Job 27:5-6).

> Where is the God of justice?
>
> (Mal. 2:17).

Thus does Scripture itself afford legitimization, in ways wholly interior to the human moral sense, for the commitment of faith. Were God the Enemy/Friend immune to the moral standards to which humankind is also subject, faith in God would simply become reprehensible. As Irving Greenberg declares, "To love someone truly is to strike a proper balance between rebuke and acceptance."[17] Ultimately speaking, the good and the right for which God stands must be identical with the good and the right for which humanity may stand. This very oneness affords humankind a self-confidence and a self-acceptance (= a victory over anxiety) together with a God-acceptance that I should beg to describe as redemptive.

Yet it is also the case, so I have argued, that the trust in God Christians may gain – essentially, their faith *means* trust – must ever remain a *questioning* faith, a *questioning* trust.

Epilogue: Some Friends of God

At the end we may add, and now quite free of ifs and buts, that the God who is Friend is loyal as well to the friends of God, even to them who fail or refuse to be God's friends.

Insofar as God is Friend, it is natural that God should seek and make friends. The scriptural company of friends of God must be counted a large one, for, as we are taught, "the Lord is near to all who call on him" (Ps. 145:18; note that the New Revised Standard Version of the Bible retains male gender identifications of God). Again, within the Psalms we encounter a remarkable union of friend, fear, and covenant:

> The friendship of the Lord is for

---

[17] Irving Greenberg, "On the Relationship of Jews and Christians and of Jews and Jews," *Jewish Action* (Winter 1990-1991), p. 26.

> those who fear him,
> and he makes his covenant
> known to them (Ps. 25:14).

Within the company friends of God, certain figures stand out. It is recorded that the Lord knew Moses "face to face" (Deut. 34:10). The Book of Isaiah has God explicitly say of Abraham that he is "my friend" (Isa. 41:8). The Letter of James is evidently carrying this particular tradition forward in the early church when it refers to Abraham as being "called the friend of God" (James 2:23). Theologically and morally speaking, who but a real friend of God would have the nerve *(chutzpah)* to remind God that God is obligated to do what is just (Gen. 18:25)? By the same reasoning, Job must have been a good friend of God (cf. Job 29:4) or he would never have been brought to protest that God seemed now to be numbering him among God's enemies. And Jesus of Nazareth must have been a close friend of God or he would not have demanded to know at the last (resorting to words of the psalmist) why God had forsaken him. Further, who but a special friend of God would be especially sent by God for purposes of human redemption?

Friends of God are found beyond the Bible. Thus is it said that Allah told Muhammad: "O Muhammad, I take you as a friend just as I took Abraham as a friend. I am speaking to you as I spoke face to face with Moses."[18]

The figures just singled out are men. Will not God as Friend have special friends who are women? The patriarchal stress of Scripture doubtless has complicating effects. Yet we are informed that male and female are equally created in the image of God (Gen. 1:27). Accordingly, the slave-girl Hagar can exclaim, "Have I really seen God and remained alive?" (Gen. 16:13). Hagar's achievement is nothing short of astonishing, for God will tell Moses: "no one shall see me and live" (Exod. 33:20; but cf. Gen. 32:30). Again, in her advanced years Sarah can be treated by God "as he had promised" and bear a child, Isaac (Gen. 21:1-3). The crossing of the Red Sea can be celebrated by Miriam, God's prophet, "and all the women" who danced and sang before the Lord (Exod. 15:19-21). Ruth of Moab can witness to Naomi that her mother-in-law's God is to be her God as well (Ruth 1:16). The prophet Jeremiah can pledge that Rachel, inconsolably weeping for her children who are no more, will one day be consoled by God (Jer. 31:15-17). Mary of Nazareth can be found, of

---

[18] As recorded in Arthur Jeffery, ed., *Islam: Muhammad and His Religion* (New York: Liberal Arts Press, 1958), p. 45.

all things, "with child from the Holy Spirit" (Matt. 1:18). And, lo and behold, it can be a lowly woman who, according to the Gospel of John, is the very first witness of the resurrected Jesus: Mary of Magdala (John 20:14-16).

In Christian history at least one band of churchpeople has ventured to go by the name Friends of God *(Gottesfreunde)*. This group, possessed of mystical inclinations, originated in the early fourteenth century within the lands of the Emperor Louis of Bavaria. Influenced by Meister Eckhart (1260-1327), their most noted member was John Tauler (1300-1361), who taught that the end of humankind is captivity by the love of God and to the love of other humans.

The authentic friend of God would appear to be friend of humankind as well. Thus are we assured that Jesus was "a friend of tax collectors and sinners" (Matt. 11:9; Luke 7:34). May not this have radical implications for the company God is resolving to keep?

The friends of God are not sinless people, for their faith ever lives under siege at the hands of their own idolatries. The friends of God are not people of certainty, for their faith is ever beset by doubt.[19] Yet in and through the continuing *metanoia* of God from Void to Enemy to Friend, from It to Thou, the Christians of this world, though not the Christians alone, are empowered to be no longer aliens, no longer strangers.

---

[19]See Paul Tillich, *Dynamics of Faith* (New York: Harper & Brothers, 1957), pp. 16-22, "Faith and Doubt."

5

Who Is This God and
What Does This God Do?

Scripture is at once cautious and audacious in what it says about God.[1]

The God Who Is A Person

The biblical story of creation is entirely silent concerning the origin of God and what God may have been about before creating this world. Yet out of such silence a testimony is forthcoming: God is not merely one more being who has happened into existence and must therefore one day cease to be. On the contrary, God is not subject to "being" but is instead the "Lord of being."[2]

> To whom then will you compare
>> me,
>> or who is my equal? says the
>> Holy One
>>
>> (Isa. 40:25).

---

[1] Is "God" a metaphor? That is to say, when people pronounce the word "God," are they thinking/acting metaphorically? There is a sense in which human words as such have a metaphorical aspect, due to the inevitable gap between language and what it is that language seeks to identify or reckon with. Yet I take it that most users of "God" are not thinking/acting metaphorically, but are proceeding rather more like someone who says, "The other day I met Paula in the drug store." The reference is to a particular person who bears the name Paula. Of course, when Christians sing, "A Mighty Fortress Is Our God," they are using "Mighty Fortress" metaphorically (= mythologically?), for they are hardly equating God with an edifice made of stone or concrete.

[2] Michael Wyschogrod, *The Body of Faith* (San Francisco: Harper & Row, 1989), pp. 101, 140; more generally, pp. 149-155.

When Moses demands to know the name of God the response is forthcoming, "I will be who I will be" (Exod. 3:13-14). God "is what he is and will be what he will be before being and nonbeing were created . . . . [The] creator of both being and nonbeing is beyond his creation and therefore beyond both being and nonbeing."[3] In the Hebraic tradition the term *Hashem* ("The Name") has long been used "to refer to God by reference to the ineffable name of God, whose pronunciation is both unknown and forbidden."[4] The proscription of uttering the name of God arises out of reverence – for God's majesty, God's holiness, God's unfathomability.

However, in Scripture God's awesome transcendence, including the transcendence of being and nonbeing, is not permitted to compromise the immanence of God.

> In his hand is the life of every
>   living thing
> and the breath of every human being
>   (Job 12:10).

To talk of the immanence of God is to enter into the question of the "personality" or "personhood" of God. Here is a piquant interpretation of "theology": taking seriously "the reality of God as a person."[5] For Reinhold Niebuhr, the "personality" or "personhood" of God connotes a height of transcendent freedom on the one hand and a relation to organic process on the other hand "that prophetic and Christian faith assumes in understanding God's transcendence over, and his immanent relation to, the world." God is at once freedom and structure.[6]

---

[3]*Ibid.*, p. 165. This statement is extremely paradoxical, since the verb "is" seems to presuppose "being." It may be said that the "isness" of God is peculiar to God and is beyond (transcends) "being" as such.

[4]*Ibid.*, p. 92. "The God of Israel is not just a Thou. *The God of Israel has a proper name.* There is no fact in Jewish theology more significant than this" (*ibid.*, p 91).

[5]*Ibid.*, p. 92.

[6]Reinhold Niebuhr, *The Nature and Destiny of Man*, vol. 2 (New York: Charles Scribner's Sons, 1943), p. 66; *The Self and the Dramas of History* (New York: Charles Scribner's Sons, 1955), p. 71. On God as both "a nature" and "a free agent," see Keith Ward, *Rational Theology and the Creativity of God* (New York: Pilgrim Press, 1982), espec. p. 165. On views upon the universe and its character by contemporary cosmologists, see John Updike, "At the Hairy Edge of the Possible," *The New Yorker*, 3 June 1991, pp. 104-108, a review-article of Alan Lightman and Roberta Brawer, eds., *Origins: The Lives and Worlds of Modern Cosmologists* (Cambridge: Harvard University Press, 1991).

To declare that God is a person is to recognize that God undergoes development in the course of the biblical story. "He creates man with certain expectations, which are apparently disappointed, and he is then sorry that he has created him. He is subject to the emotions of anger and jealousy, among others. He is also filled with burning love, particularly toward Abraham and his descendants. He desires certain things and detests others. He is faithful in the sense of keeping his promises, even when for long periods of time it seems that he has forgotten them and has no intention of keeping them." Scripture is telling us of "a passionate and concerned God who is a real . . . person and who stands in personal relation with many human beings."[7] God addresses humankind, and humankind may in turn address God.

The transcendent/immanent God of the Bible is not a disembodied principle or idea, not a spiritual essence contemplating its own navel, but is instead a doer, i.e., One who pursues a life of action, of deeds. In David Birnbaum's luxuriant phrasing: "Holy quest for potential – our parallel to the kabbalistic *En Sof* [The Limitless One] – is the 'primal scream' of the cosmos. Holy Potential, emanating through and from the Divine essence, radiates through the universe – questing, pulsating, exploding, reaching, energizing, expanding, in time and out-of-time."[8]

The Life-Struggle of God

The friendship of God for humanity is made visible and coherent in and through the praxis of God: God's life-struggle, God's acts of compassion, God's deeds of humility. We consider these three themes in succession; they are interwoven.

In and through God's combat with humankind as sinner, as in God's combat with other evil forces (the Devil? the demonic?), clues are given to God as Enemy and also as Friend, the God who hates sin yet loves the sinner, the God who hates the world's evil yet loves the world.

None of this lets God off the hook. Shattering queries are addressed to the God who is the person accountable for every macrocosm and every microcosm: Why must I suffer? Why do my people suffer? Why is there evil? Why is there *so much* evil? Why is there such terrible and terrifying evil? (Only an impersonal deity is exempt, mercifully, from such questions, such accusations.) The

---

[7]Wyschogrod, *Body of Faith*, pp. 84, 104.
[8]David Birnbaum, *God and Evil* (Hoboken: Ktav Publishing Company, 1989), p. 78.

people of God are here propelled into the life-struggle of God. They find themselves enmeshed in that struggle. In the wording of Harold M. Schulweis, "the Gothic word 'evil' refers to the force in the universe that gives rise to wickedness, sin, misfortune, disaster. The presence of evil, its reality, makes a hole in the heart of the believer."[9]

The traditional word for human strivings to vindicate God's-justice-and-righteousness-amidst-the-reality-of-evil is "theodicy." I fear that all such attempts, however well-intentioned, are crushed under the elephantine divine blameworthiness. The pages that immediately follow spell out this state of affairs.

In illustration of the misadventure of theodicy – its brave but, in the end, abortive effort to disperse *(zerstieben)* God as Enemy – I make reference to expositions of the Christian theologian S. Paul Schilling and the Jewish theologian David Birnbaum. These apologists are united by the contention that the reality of evil may be "justified" in and through the indispensable divine goal and essential value of freedom.

Schilling is uncomfortable with any "belief in the determination of all events by the divine will" and instead puts himself on the side of the "increasing numbers" of theologians (and scientists) who have come to "assign to randomness a positive role in creation and affirm a complementarity of chance and law." Schilling is in accord with David J. Bartholomew's reasoning that (in Schilling's words) "God's goal for human life could not be obtained without human freedom; but if there is to be scope for the operation of real freedom, creation must provide for genuine uncertainty. The presence of chance in the universe, therefore, instead of leaving no room for God, is rather an important means whereby divine purposes are attained." As Bartholomew puts the matter, the occurrence of events that God does not intend "goes a long way toward reconciling undeserved suffering with the love of God." Schilling concludes that to acknowledge the role of chance within a purposive, orderly structure is to offer at least a partial answer "to the problem of reconciling belief in divine goodness with the realities of evil and suffering."[10]

The difficulty with this argument is that the exalted purposes of God – for example, to create and sustain a free humankind – can do

---

[9]Harold M. Schulweis, *Evil and the Morality of God* (Cincinnati: Hebrew Union College Press, 1984), p. 1.
[10]S. Paul Schilling, "Chance and Order in Science and Theology," *Theology Today* 47 (1991): 369, 370, 376; David J. Bartholomew, *God of Chance* (London: SCM Press, 1984), p. 145.

nothing whatsoever to exempt God from ultimate blameworthiness
for evil (as an intrinsic element within God's responsibility for all
things[11]).

On his part, David Birnbaum is rendering a contemporary
version, but an original and comprehensive one, of the historic,
mystical kabbalist idea of the contraction or retreat *(tsimtsum)* of
the God who is omnipotent and just, for the sake of, and in essential
correlation with, the "very existence of the world" and, more
especially, the prosperity of human freedom. Birnbaum labels his
position a "neo-kabbalistic development."[12]

Birnbaum surely faces up to the evil of evil in all its fullness:
"How can we affirm the validity of a sincere religious commitment in
a world where we ourselves have witnessed such prevalence of
gratuitous, gross evil? The problem goes beyond the issue of the
suffering of the innocent, and beyond the question of the suffering of
the righteous. It involves the fundamental issue of whether there is
any higher moral order at all to the cosmos . . . . To insist on classic
individual Providence for the Jewish children of Europe is simply to
imply a God-turned-satanic controlling the cosmos." However,
Birnbaum is at the same time assured that he has the answer to the
problem, an answer he finds "implicit in the biblical text." Here is
"the core" of his theodicy:

1.   The purpose of man is to quest for his potential – spiritual and
     other.
2.   The greater man's freedom, the greater his ability to attain his
     potential.
3.   Freedom requires privacy, responsibility, and selfhood.
4.   In order to yield man greater freedom . . ., God has contracted
     His here-and-now consciousness [= infinitude], in correlation to
     mankind's ascent in knowledge.
5.   With the Divine consciousness increasingly contracted from the
     here-and-now, and evil existent in the here-and-now, man is
     increasingly forced to confront evil on his own.

With the creation of a potential for growth and for good,
required as this is if humankind is to reach its spiritual potential
(here is where Providence enters, understood in its larger meaning),
the potential for evil – indirectly but yet inexorably (Birnbaum here
follows Moses Maimonides) – "came into its existence as a
consequence." (Query: Why must this consequence follow?) Humanity
"cannot demand both complete personal freedom with concomitant

[11] Schilling does concede that "all that happens is ultimately God's
responsibility" ("Chance and Order," p. 371).
[12] Birnbaum, *God and Evil*, pp. 68, 98, 127, 141.

privacy, and, at the same time, a God who intervenes when peril threatens." It is by allowing humankind "to develop in freedom and reach its fullest cosmic potentialities" that God "manifests His care and concern" for human beings. One implication of all this is that God becomes "somewhat dependent" upon humanity. "If there were no potential for tragedy, there would be no potential for triumph or growth. The two come wrapped inextricably together. And if there were no potential for growth and quest for ultimate potentiality, there might have been no creation at all. No triumph at all. No stars at all. No children at all. No love at all. No laughter at all. Literally."[13] (Query: Why not?)

Birnbaum apprehends the "proportional contraction" of God's presence as a primary form of *Hester Panim* (the Hiding of God's Face, or what Joseph B. Soloveitchik defines as a "temporary suspension of God's active surveillance"), as put forward by numbers of theologians. *Hester Panim* and variations thereon are found in a number of scriptural verses (Deut. 31: 17-18; Isa. 1:12; 8:17; 45:15; 54:8; 57:17; 59:2; 64:7; Job 34:29). While *Hester Panim* is often occasioned by human sin, Eliezer Berkovits comments that "the Divine Presence could reveal itself only from behind some protective barrier, or else man could not have survived the 'terror' of the Almighty."[14] This latter judgment is not unreminiscent of our own earlier retention of God as Enemy.

Crucial to Birnbaum's position is his assent to the view – nowhere really demonstrated by him – that "evil has to exist as a counterpart to the good," yet an acknowledgment he makes strictly within the context of the question, "Why does not omnipotent, omnimerciful God intervene to counter gross evil?" "Good and evil form a duality. Creating potential for good, by definition, creates the inverse potential for evil along with it. Good only exists with its duality, evil. In order to create potential for good, potential for evil was, by definition, created. God's omnipotence or non-omnipotence is not the issue. It is rather a question of definition. By definition, good comes packaged with concomitant evil." (Query: Who in the world has bestowed such high authority upon "definition"? I should think that evil is much more a mystery than our philosopher here permits.)

We are counseled that God "is not sitting outside the crematorium watching while infants are being burned alive." That would be an

---

[13]*Ibid.*, pp. xx, 147, 153, 54, 62, 146, 215, 115, 74, 155-156.
[14]*Ibid.*, pp. 16, 117-118, 124, 129; Eliezer Berkovits, *God, Man and History* (Middle Village, N.Y.: Jonathan David, 1959), pp. 145-146.

abomination to *El Moleh Rachamim,* a God full of mercy. No, "it must be presumed that God is in a state of contracted real-time consciousness for the higher purpose, elected by man, of allowing the totality of infants and men to grow up in a state of bona fide personal freedom, so that they may grasp for the totality of their potentialities." Yet Birnbaum himself hesitates, adding: "The price, however, is often high, too high."[15]

I suggest that David Birnbaum's hesitation could have been turned into something more bold and constructive, more radical (*radix,* the root). He could – as could S. Paul Schilling – have transcended his own explanatory (philosophic) reasoning. For as matters stand he fails to come to terms with the divine blameworthiness in its final depth. Near the start of our fourth chapter, Eliezer Berkovits is quoted; I repeat his remorseless words: "God is responsible for having created a world in which man is free to make history." In addition, let us listen to Emil L. Fackenheim:

> The pious men of a *shtibl* in the Lodz Ghetto spent a whole day fasting, praying, reciting psalms, and then, having opened the holy ark, convoked a solemn *din Torah* [legal hearing], and forbade God to punish his people any further. (Elsewhere God was put on trial – and found guilty.) And in the Warsaw Ghetto a handful of Jews, ragged, alone, poorly armed, carried out the first uprising against the Holocaust Kingdom in all of Europe. The rabbis showed religious piety when, rather than excuse God or curse him, they cited his own promises against him. The fighters showed secular piety when, rather than surrender to the Satanic Kingdom, they took up arms against it. The common element in these two responses was not hope but rather despair. To the rabbis who found him guilty, the God who had broken his promises in the Holocaust could no longer be trusted to keep *any* promise, the messianic included. And precisely when hope had come to an end the fighters took to arms in a rebellion that had no hope of succeeding.[16]

The issue that counts is not the explanation of the reality of evil.[17] Such endeavors may achieve relative degrees of success or

---

[15]Birnbaum, *God and Evil,* pp. 33, 194, 95, 163-164. Cf. Isaiah 45:7:

> I form light and create darkness,
>
> I make weal and create woe;
>
> I the Lord do all these things.

[16]Emil L. Fackenheim, *The Jewish Return Into History: Reflections in the Age of Auschwitz and a New Jerusalem* (New York: Schocken Books, 1978), pp. 281-282.

[17]If the Bible is silent upon the "origin" of God, it is prevailingly silent upon the origins of evil (but cf., e.g., Isa. 45:7; Eph. 6:11-12). Whatever the sources and "rationale" of evil, certain it is that God is engaged in a life-and-death

failure. Driven by a world of mass human executions and other diabolic evils, the question that stays with us is: Who ultimately bears the responsibility (*Verantwortlichkeit*, accountability + *Strafbarkeit*, culpability) for a universe in which gross Evil plays so pervasive and horrible a role? Here is the fateful difficulty in Birnbaum's moral logic: To contend that evil "has to exist" as a counterpart to good is to do nothing at all to neutralize or even offset God's responsibility for the reality of evil.

There is, accordingly, much irony in Birnbaum's own allusion to the episode in the Lodz Ghetto, for he has to concede that what the protestors did was to invoke "the logic of theodicy back on itself."[18] Exactly here lies the point: We can scarcely allow the place of God and of God's accountability to be filled, in effect, by Freedom! Several pages earlier I express the fear that attempts at "theodicy" are crushed by the divine blameworthiness. Accordingly, if there is to be any reconciliation of God's guilt and God's goodness, this will have to emerge from "beyond theodicy." Put differently: *No one ever forced, or could force, God to create a cosmos. No one ever forced, or could force, God to retreat from the dimension of here-and-now consciousness. And, as we reminded ourselves in chapter two, no human being ever has anything to say about their very own existence – not excepting the human devils who organize and run death camps.* Thus is consigned to the moral rubbish heap any apology according to which the *Shoah* and untold numbers of comparable events constitute the sin and guilt of humankind but not equally the sin and guilt of God.[19]

We have been directed back to the question of blame-and-accountability as this is raised in chapter four. To affirm that God is engaged in a struggle, a struggle to resolve conflicts that are monumental and cosmic, gains moral authority and makes moral sense only upon the ground of God's full accountability and culpability. If there is to be any response from a righteous God to the unqualifiedly justified accusation of God's guilt, it may be put forward, not via the dazzlements of philosophic reckoning, but only from within the domain of God's own life and praxis. Otherwise, we are left marooned upon the desert island of God's enmity. To go "beyond theodicy," as we must, is to make clear the shortcomings of theodicy yet still to witness (here David Birnbaum is on the right track) that

---

struggle with evil. To speak of God's struggle with evil is to express the negative side of a positive intention: to vindicate justice and righteousness.
[18] Birnbaum, *God and Evil*, p. 10.
[19] A. Roy Eckardt, *For Righteousness' Sake* (Bloomington: Indiana University Press, 1987), p. 317; in general, pp. 315-325.

the God/humanity encounter is, in the end, *morally* intelligible.[20] But such moral intelligibility can only derive from God's own justification of Godself *in and through certain ongoing events in the divine history* that convey the repentance *(teshuvah, metanoia)*, the compassion, indeed the saving humiliation of God. What is it that God the Friend of humans *does* before the fact of God as Enemy? (Why does God forsake humanity? Yet why does God not forsake humanity?)

The One Who Is Compassion[21]

Abraham Joshua Heschel points the way: "The preoccupation with justice, the passion with which the [biblical] prophets condemn injustice, is rooted in their sympathy with divine pathos. The chief characteristic of prophetic thought is the primacy of God's involvement in history. History is the domain with which the prophets' minds are occupied." The prophet knows that above and beyond God's judgment and above and beyond God's anger stands God's mercy.[22] ("Pathos" is linked to the Greek *paschein*, to suffer.)

The personal God, who appears as a dynamic reality doing battle with evil, is a God of love and compassion, overflowing with righteousness and sworn to profit justice.

> The Lord of hosts is exalted
>> by justice,
> and the Holy God proves himself
>> holy by righteousness
>>> (Isa. 5:16).

(Is not a reversion implied: no righteousness, no holiness?)

Even when Israel falls into sin the covenant stands fast:

> "And I will have pity on Not pitied,
>> and I will say to Not my people,
>>> 'You are my people';

---

[20] See e.g., Birnbaum, *God and Evil*, p. 45. For a study that places greater stress upon the Hebrew Bible than does Birnbaum, consult Jon D. Levenson, *Creation and the Persistence of Evil: The Jewish Drama of Divine Omnipotence* (San Francisco: Harper & Row, 1988).

[21] This section partially applies but also goes beyond Eckardt, *For Righteousness' Sake*, pp. 25-29.

[22] Abraham Joshua Heschel, *The Prophets*, vol. 1 (New York: Harper Colophon Books, 1969), pp. 218-219, 23.

and he shall say, 'Thou art my
   God'"

                                (Hos. 2:23, *RSV*).

How can I give you up, O Ephraim!
   How can I hand you over, O Israel! . . .
My heart recoils within me,
   My compassion grows warm and tender.
I will not execute my fierce anger,
   I will not again destroy Ephraim;
for I am God and not man,
   the Holy One in your midst,
   and I will not come to destroy

                              (Hos. 11:8-9, *RSV*).

It is, indeed, through God's love and mercy that Israel is chosen in the first place. Walter Harrelson finds biblical-Hebraic usage giving "great force to the theological point" that "God's mercy precedes his laying down of the covenant requirements." Thus do the Ten Commandments or Ten Words (Decalogue) themselves arise "in a context of divine grace." The Decalogue is, in actuality, Israel's "great charter of freedom."[23] One is reminded of the prayer said every day by the believing Jew: "Our Father, our King, be gracious unto us, for we have no works. Save us according to thy grace."

    Through the compassion of God the divine repentance is authorized:

This is what the Lord God showed me: he was forming locusts at the time the latter growth began to sprout (it was the latter growth after the king's mowings). When they had finished eating the grass of the land, I said,

"O Lord God, forgive, I beg you!
   How can Jacob stand?
   He is so small!"
The Lord relented concerning
   this;
"It shall not be," said the Lord.

This is what the Lord God showed me: the Lord God was calling for a shower of fire, and it devoured the great deep and was eating up the land. Then I said,

"O Lord God, cease, I beg you!

---

[23]Walter Harrelson, *The Ten Commandments and Human Rights* (Philadelphia: Fortress Press, 1980), pp. 46, 20.

> How can Jacob stand?
> He is so small!"
The Lord relented concerning this:
> "This also shall not be," said
>> the Lord God

(Amos 7:1-6).

In Bernhard W. Anderson's explication, "for Isaiah, as for the other prophets, the experience of the holy is not an encounter with mysterious, numinous power wholly beyond the mundane sphere where human beings struggle to find meaning and fulfillment in society. Isaiah stands firmly in the Mosaic tradition which testified to the in-breaking of divine holiness into the world with redemptive concern and ethical demand . . . . The holiness of Yahweh, then, is manifest as saving power directed toward the realization of justice/righteousness."[24] Accordingly: "Thus says the Lord: Do not let the wise boast in their wisdom, do not let the mighty boast in their might, do not let the wealthy boast in their wealth; but let those who boast boast in this, that they understand and know me, that I am the Lord; I act with steadfast love, justice, and righteousness in the earth, for in these things I delight, says the Lord" (Jer. 9:23-24).

So devoted is God to love/justice/righteousness that God is brought to tears before the wickedness of God's people:

You shall say to them this word:

Let my eyes run down with tears
> night and day,
> and let them not cease,
for the virgin daughter – my
>> people – is struck down
>> with a crushing blow,
> with a very grievous wound

(Jer. 14:17).

Finally, the divine compassion discerned by the prophets is matched in the Psalms. Perhaps best known as a perennial response to God's deliverance of Israel from Egypt is the chant of Ps. 136, wherein the antiphonal wording, "for his steadfast love endures forever," is many times repeated. Again, this delivering God, who

---

[24]Bernhard W. Anderson, *The Eighth Century Prophets: Amos-Hosea-Isaiah-Micah* (Philadelphia: Fortress Press, 1978), pp. 66-67. In Birnbaum's phrasing, the relation between God and humankind "is not relegated to . . . unfathomable domains" (*God and Evil*, p. 37).

for the sake of righteousness must judge and condemn, nevertheless
forgives:

> If you, O Lord, should mark iniquities,
>> Lord, who could stand?
> But there is forgiveness with you,
>> so that you may be revered (Ps. 130:3-4).

> The Lord is merciful and gracious,
>> slow to anger and abounding
>>> in steadfast love (Ps. 103:8).

Human faith reaches a redeeming height whenever humankind
is made genuinely sorry for God (*daath elohim,* sympathy for God). In
this way the human face may hide itself from the making of
repeated accusations against God.

It is not that the tears of God console; there can be no consolation
for such terrors as the *Shoah.* Instead, what the tears of God do is to
declare that human beings are not alone.[25] Planet Earth and Galaxy
NGC 1232 are moved into the one neighborhood, and they are made
friends. As for the people of God, no longer are they aliens, no longer
are they strangers.

The One Who Humbles Godself

The compassion and the suffering of God cross over into and abide
within the discretely Christian dispensation. The structure they take
on, or the body, is Jesus Christ.[26] Jesus is the stranger who yet comes
to Christians as their friend.

All Christian apprehension of the deed or deeds of God in Jesus
Christ rests upon John 3:16: "For God so loved the world that he gave
his only Son, so that everyone who believes in him may not perish
but may have eternal life."

The second part of this verse has been an influential basis of
exclusivist claims for Christianity, oftentimes involving the
contention that unless people are Christians they will not be

---

[25] Cf. Abraham Joshua Heschel, *Man is Not Alone* (New York: Farrar, Strauss
& Young, 1951).
[26] On recent Christology, consult A. Roy Eckardt, *Reclaiminq the Jesus of
History: Christology Today* (Minneapolis: Fortress Press, 1992); Jacquelyn Grant,
*White Women's Christ and Black Women's Jesus: Feminist Christology and
Womanist Response* (Atlanta: Scholars Press, 1989); Elizabeth A. Johnson,
Consider Jesus: Waves of Renewal in Christology (London: Geoffrey Chapman,
1990); and Jürgen Moltmann, *The Way of Jesus Christ: Christology in Messianic
Dimensions* (San Francisco: Harper: SanFrancisco, 1990).

"saved." However, the first part of the verse almost seems to stand in judgment upon such exclusivism, particularly when the love of God is rendered in the way Paul attests in I Corinthians 13 (called by H. Richard Niebuhr a portrait of Jesus Christ): "Love is patient, love is kind; love is not envious or boastful or arrogant or rude. It does not insist upon its own way . . ." (I Cor. 13:4-5).

The humility/humiliation of God reaches a zenith in Paul's Letter to the Philippians:[27]

> Let the same mind be in you
> that was in Christ Jesus,
>> who, though he was in the form of God,
>> did not regard equality with God
>> as something to be exploited,
> but emptied himself [*heauton ekenose*],
>> taking the form of a slave,
>> being born in human likeness.
> And being found in human form,
>> he humbled himself
>> and became obedient to the
>>> point of death –
>> even death on a cross.
>
> Therefore God also highly exalted him
>> and gave him the name
>> that is above every name,
> so that at the name of Jesus
>> every knee should bend,
>> in heaven and on earth
>>> and under the earth,
> and every tongue should confess
>> that Jesus Christ is Lord,
>> to the glory of God the Father
>>>> (Phil. 2:5-11).

Two questions confront us. First, does not Paul here anticipate the same absolutist claim for the Christian faith which seems to mark the second part of John 3:16? Second, could it be that Paul here treats the act of "emptying" (*kenosis*) as some kind of human achievement?[28]

---

[27] Many scholars maintain that this passage is pre-Pauline.
[28] There is no way to show that Jesus was perfectly, exclusively, and uninterruptedly committed or devoted to God and the Kingdom of God. We

We consider the issue of Christian exclusivism in chapter 7. Suffice it to say for the moment that recent Christian thinking has entailed a considerable move away from Christian absolutism. The claims of Christianity tend instead to be treated as confessional in character, directed in the first instance within the Christian community of faith.

The second question puts before us several choices: that *kenosis* in "Christ Jesus" was a human attainment, that it was strictly God's act, that it was a combination of these. The Apostle Paul sometimes suggests a kind of synergism as between God's grace and human strength, e.g., in his counsel to the Philippians (immediately following the above passage), "work out your own salvation with fear and trembling, for it is God who is at work in you, enabling you both to will and to work for his good pleasure" (Phil. 2:12-13). Yet the primacy of God's empowering grace is here made evident, with the human will as a subordinate, if integral, factor. Paul's rendering of the Christian faith is anything but anthropocentric; it is theocentric. The point is that, apart from the presence and power of God, "Christ Jesus" could never have "emptied himself" and taken "the form of a slave" (or servant). This means, in the final resort, that it is God who empties Godself. Or, as John Macquarrie describes kenotic thinking, this viewpoint stands for the "self-emptying of the Logos [Word of God], whereby it was able to manifest itself in the finite life of a human being."[29]

We are here met by the Incarnation of God in Jesus Christ.

Paul writes to the church in Corinth, "we proclaim Jesus Christ as Lord and ourselves as your slaves for Jesus' sake. For it is the God who said, 'Let light shine out of darkness,' who has shone in our hearts to give the light of the knowledge of the glory of God in the face of Jesus Christ" (I Cor. 4: 5-6). We are reminded, by contrast, of *Hester Panim*, the Hiding of God's Face. However, no less devout a Christian thinker than Søren Kierkegaard sees in the Incarnation not alone a genuine renunciation or emptying *(kenosis)* but also a hiding or hiddenness *(krypsis)*. As Macquarrie points out, few Christian scholars of today would agree with Kierkegaard that Jesus declared

---

simply do not have the information to support such a claim. But kenotic thinking does not rest its case upon human achievement, even that of Jesus. It directs us to the loving action and grace of God.

[29] John Macquarrie, *Jesus Christ in Modern Thought* (London: SCM Press; Philadelphia: Trinity Press International, 1990), p. 245; in general, pp. 245-250.

he was God[30] – much less that he *was* God. The conviction that God was incarnate *in* Jesus Christ is quite another matter.

Kierkegaard is reverting to incarnation doctrine when he declares: "God's servant-form . . . is not a mere disguise, but is actual . . . from the hour that in the omnipotent purpose of his omnipotent love, God became a servant, he has, so to speak, imprisoned himself in his resolve, and is now bound to go on (to speak foolishly) whether it pleases him or no . . . . God's presence in human form, aye in the humble form of a servant, is itself the teaching . . ." – to which Macquarrie adds that "we seem to have advanced beyond *krypsis*, 'hiding' or 'disguise,' to *kenosis*, 'emptying' . . . ."[31] As Paul has it, God "reconciled us to himself through Christ, and has given us the ministry of reconciliation; that is, in Christ God was reconciling the world to himself, not counting their trespasses against them, and entrusting the message of reconciliation to us. So we are ambassadors for Christ, since God is making his appeal through us; we entreat you on behalf of Christ, be reconciled to God. For our sake he made him to be sin who knew no sin, so that in him we might become the righteousness of God" (2 Cor. 5:18-21).

The end-place of God's *kenosis* is the lowliness and mortification of Jesus Christ.

"Is not this the carpenter's son?"
(Matt. 13:54).

"The Son of Man came not to be served
but to serve" (Matt. 20:28).

As he came near and saw the city,
he wept over it (Luke 19:41).

"This is my body, which is given for you"
(Luke 22:19).

Then he poured water into a basin and began to wash the disciples' feet and to wipe them with the towel that was tied around him (John 13:5).

And they crucified him, and divided his

---

[30]*Ibid.,* pp. 245, 241, 242. Macquarrie apprehends the great majority of Christian theologians as holding that "Christ is God," but "understanding the 'is' in the sense of predication rather than identity." The reverse wording, "God is Jesus," would be rejected by most theologians as improperly restrictive of "God" (*ibid.,* p. 258).

[31]Søren Kierkegaard, *Philosophical Fragments or a Fragment of Philosophy,* trans. David E. Swenson (Princeton: Princeton University Press, 1944), p. 44; Macquarrie, *Jesus Christ,* p. 242.

clothes among them, casting lots to
decide what each should take

(Mark 15:24).

Though he was rich, yet for your sakes
he became poor, so that by his
poverty you might become rich

(2 Cor. 8:9).

Although he was a Son, he learned
obedience through what he suffered

(Heb. 5:8).

A conclusion of Jürgen Moltmann may be called upon for summary purposes here: There is no loneliness and no rejection that God has not taken to Godself in the Cross of Jesus.[32]

At the place of the Incarnation, Christianity is usually held to part company with Judaism. However, the discontinuity is not total or unqualified. I include three citations, one from the Christian John Macquarrie and one each from the Jewish thinkers, Norman Lamm and Michael Wyschogrod.

> *Almost* every mention of God *(Theos)* in the New Testament refers to the traditional God of Israel, not to Jesus Christ or to the Holy Spirit. This word "God" and what it stands for was a necessary presupposition for any Christian assertions such as that Christ had been sent by God or was the Son of God or was the Word of God or even was God. Yet if Christ was the Word of God . . . then there is a reciprocity between the Hebrew inheritance and the revelation in Christ. Only the inherited understanding of God permitted the disciples to say Christ had come from God, yet as soon as this was said, it meant that God must be understood anew in the light of Christ, as his own self-communication (Macquarrie).

> God is especially immanent in Torah, and the study of Torah is therefore a means of achieving an encounter with the divine Presence . . . . Torah, as such, is far more than a document of the divine legislation; it is in itself, mystically, an aspect of God (Lamm).

> [If man] is to have a relation to Hashem [The Name] . . . then Hashem must be able to enter space and to be near man wherever he is. And not only near man but in man, or more specifically, in the people of Israel (Wyschogrod).[33]

---

[32] Jürgen Moltmann, *The Crucified God,* trans. R. A. Wilson and John Bowden (New York: Harper & Row, 1974), p. 277. See also Moltmann, *The Way of Jesus Christ,* chap. 4, "The Apocalyptic Sufferings of Christ."
[33] Macquarrie, *Jesus Christ,* p. 378; Norman Lamm, as cited by Birnbaum, *God and Evil,* p. 243; Wyschogrod, *Body of Faith,* p. 101.

All through the story of Judaism, God as Enemy is transfigured by the historical deeds of God as Friend. For Christians, the human alienation that is tied to God as Enemy is transfigured by God's acceptance of people in and through the gift of Jesus Christ.

Emil L. Fackenheim alludes to a Talmudic ambiguity upon the hiding of God:[34] "Does [God] hide in wrath against, or punishment of, His people? God forbid that He should do so at such a time [as ours]! Does He hide for reasons unknown? God forbid that He should, in this of all times, be a *deus absconditus* [a secretive or obscuring God]! Then why does He hide?" It is his weeping that he hides. "He hides His weeping in the inner chamber, for *just as God is infinite so His pain is infinite, and this, were it to touch the world, would destroy it . . . . God so loved the world that He hid the infinity of His pain from it lest it be destroyed. . . .*"[35]

As Christians hear these words they hear as well John 3:16: "For God so loved the world that he gave his only Son . . . ." At this juncture, there is manifest in all its starkness the *Auseinandersetzung* (place of sundering) or perhaps the denouement of the Jewish-and-Christian reality. In language earlier used: Here is found, but now in excruciating form, the dialectic between hiding *(krypsis)* and emptying *(kenosis)*.

Is the chasm uncrossable? Many have said yes and many will say yes. But wherever the love of God is present, the chasm is crossed – from each of the two directions. For it is in the hiding that the love of God is given; and it is in the giving that the love of God is hidden. "Jesus said: 'Let the little children come to me, and do not stop them; for it is to such as these that the kingdom of heaven belongs.' And he laid his hands on them and went his way" (Matt. 19:14-15). John F. Kennedy said, "What really matters is the children" – who not only are not responsible for their own birth but have not come to the age of culpable destructiveness. Were the infinity of God's pain to touch the world, the world would indeed be destroyed. Accordingly, God must empty Godself, continuing to weep within the inner chamber (as God once wept beneath the Cross). In the meantime God may address humankind as a whole in and through the small children of the world. This is to suggest that in the long run, however guilty God appears, God is innocent, as the children are innocent. God does not willfully sin. God does the best

---

[31]This and the ensuing two paragraphs are adapted from A. Roy Eckardt, *Reclaiming the Jesus of History,* pp. 222-223.
[35]Emil L. Fackenheim, *What Is Judaism? An Interpretation for the Present Age* (New York: Summit Books, 1987), p. 291.

that God can: this is the crux of faith. Therefore it is fitting that in Elie Wiesel's *Twilight*, Raphael should at the end reject the idea that God could be cruel.[36]

The specter of gross evil is meaningfully and decisively confronted, not by humanly-contrived theodicies, but by the *behavior* of God. As God weeps, so may human beings weep.[37] As God forgives, so may human beings forgive. It is a pity when persons go through life carrying secret grudges against God, never quite pardoning God for one or another catastrophe or experience of suffering. Yet to God the Enemy it ever remains possible to say, "We forgive you." Now may the Enemy become Thou. And then may the aliens be no longer aliens, the strangers no longer strangers.

The God Who Is One-In-Three

As made plain at the start of this book, some facets of the Christian faith are not discussed herein. However, as we near the end of our discrete representations of God, a special word is in order upon the central teaching of the Trinity. As intimated in the following citation, that subject has been with us throughout, if the specific terminology has been lacking.

Robert McAfee Brown recreates an imaginary early church council or perhaps simply a discussion over coffee at the First Church of Ephesus:

Topic: "Who is the God we worship?"

First answer: We worship the God of our fathers [and mothers], the God of Abraham, Isaac, and Jacob [and Sarah, Leah, and Rachel], who always has been and always will be.

Second answer: Amen to all that, with the addition that it is *that very same God* who has drawn near to us, entered into and shared our lot in Jesus of Nazareth, to enact, rather than just talk about, God's love for us. This is one reason we have kept the Hebrew Scriptures as part of our own sacred writings, so that nobody will miss the connection.

---

[36] Elie Wiesel *Twilight*, trans. Marion Wiesel (New York: Summit Books, 1988), p. 211.
[37] In the course of *Tikkun Hatzot*, certain prayers are recited at midnight, in mourning for the destruction of the Temple and the Jewish state. These were instituted in the 16th century by a kabbalist group in Safed. Emil L. Fackenheim has alluded to the Talmudic story of how at midnight God weeps, and of how some 1000 years afterward the tradition took hold among pious Jews of weeping with God. To this time, it is told, a certain man in a certain Canadian city rises every night to weep with God (from an oral account by Fackenheim).

Third answer: Amen once again, to both these claims, with the addition that it is that same God-of-our-ancestors-also-revealed-in-Jesus-of Nazareth whose presence we feel *here and now,* day after day, and especially when we gather to break bread and share wine. The breath of God, God's spirit, empowers us and makes God our contemporary.

Program chairperson: Anybody taking notes? Let's get it written down: one God (not three) in three manifestations (not two or five).[38]

Epilogue: A Philosophic Word

Although this book is not a philosophic study, I think we may reason that the biblical teaching of God's transcendence/immanence, together with God's personhood, is congruent with the theory of panentheism (*not* pantheism). We should not say that God and "all things" are one, but rather that "all things" somehow fall "inside" the being of God (God as immanent). Yet God's immanence is not absolute (as in pantheism); God continues to transcend "all things."

From a panentheist perspective the pain and the suffering that this world's creatures bring to one another and experience independently (e.g., through disease) do not fall outside the reality, or maybe one could even say the body, of God.[39] Hence, such phenomena are not wholly meaningless or dispurposive, and we may respond to them in other than despairing or cynical ways. Yet if there is divine care for creatures such that their suffering can or will be redeemed, this still takes place in ways that are obscured to human beings.

In this chapter we have not addressed the question of the Resurrection of Jesus Christ. That subject will arise in the course of chapters 8 and 9.

---

[38] Robert McAfee Brown, "Thinking About God," *Christianity and Crisis* 51 (1991): 164.
[39] Sallie McFague describes the world as "God's body" (*Metaphorical Theology: Models of God in Religious Language* [Philadelphia: Fortress Press, 1982], p. 61); see also her *Models of God* (Philadelphia: Fortress Press, 1987), pp. 69-78; and Grace Jantzen, *God's World, God's Body* (Philadelphia: Westminster Press, 1984).

Part II

CHRISTIAN TEACHINGS:
MORAL RESPONSIBILITY AND DAILY
DECISION-MAKING

6

What, Then, Are These
Christians To Do?, Part I

Alienation from God, the world, and humankind begins to be assuaged whenever and wherever human beings take up responsibility for the life of God, of the world, of humanity.[1] Because human earthlings have no say in their own existence, this Yes of responsibility may be received as a beneficent Yes to creation, even as a work of supererogation, even as an exercise in grace. (Yet since grace is a gift of God, the taking of responsibility cannot be a matter of human merit alone.)

---

[1]Consult James D. Davidson, C. Lincoln Johnson, and Alan K. Mock, eds., *Faith and Social Ministry: Ten Christian Perspectives* (Chicago: Loyola University Press, 1990), which examines the relationship among faith, social ministry, and their interconnections as put forward among ten American denominations; Gary J. Dorrien, *Reconstructing the Common Good: Theology and the Social Order* (Maryknoll, N.Y.: Orbis Books, 1990), dealing with the history and theory of modern Christian socialism; Duncan B. Forrester, *Theology and Politics* (Oxford: Basil Blackwell, 1988), containing much on liberation theology, political theology, and a political Christ; Rowland A. Sherrill, ed., *Religion and the Life of the Nation* (Urbana: University of Illinois Press, 1990), which examines the role that religion has played and plays in American culture; Susan Brooks Thistlethwaite and Mary Potter Engels, eds., *Lift Every Voice: Constructing Christian Theologies from the Underside* (San Francisco: Harper & Row, 1990), a combining of contemporary liberation and feminist thinking from around the world; Glenn Tinder, *The Political Meaning of Christianity* (Baton Rouge-London: Louisiana State University Press, 1989), wherein it is argued that a truly prophetic Christian understanding of and action upon politics ought to be God-centered; and Sharon D. Welch, *A Feminist Ethic of Risk* (Minneapolis: Fortress Press, 1989), which grapples with the question of working "for social transformation in the face of seemingly insurmountable suffering and evil."

Faith and Works

In this study we are seeking to reason our way through and to cope with the meaning and reality of human faith, more particularly the Christian faith. Yet faith is not necessarily a "good" thing.

A nationwide inquiry conducted by the General Council on Ministries of the United Methodist Church shows that three out of four of the denomination's female clergy have experienced sexual harassment, 41 percent reporting that the harassment came from other ministers. Again, the notion that once individual people are "saved" in or by Jesus Christ, they will behave in higher moral fashion is not perforce correct. Ever aware as we may be of Amnon Hadary's contention that statistical documentation is a "demogogic technique," we can hardly ignore a recent poll by the Roper organization, which found that while 4 percent of born-again Christians admitted to drunken driving before being converted, three times as many owned up to such behavior after conversion. Five percent acknowledged using illegal drugs before conversion, 9 percent after. And adultery more than doubled: 2 percent before, 5 percent after.[2]

From the Christian point of view put forward in this book, the claims that religion makes are subject to assessment at the hands of moral action.

The foundation of Christian morality is suffusedly biblical and Hebraic. We have cited Jeremiah upon the inseparability of love/justice/righteousness in God: "I act with steadfast love, justice, and righteousness in the earth." Again:

> You shall love your neighbor as yourself
> (Lev. 19:18).

> Is not this the fast that I choose:
>   to loose the bands of injustice,
>   to undo the thongs of the yoke,
> to let the oppressed go free,
>   and to break every yoke? (Isa. 58:6).
> I hate, I despise your feasts,
>   and I take no delight in your
>   solemn assemblies . . . .
> But let justice roll down like
>   waters,

---

[2]Ari L. Goldman, "Religion Notes," *The New York Times,* 1 December 1990; "Backsliding Born Again," *The Christian Century* 107 (1990): 990.

and righteousness like an
everflowing stream (Amos 5:24).
He has told you, O mortal, what
is good;
and what does the Lord
require of you
but to do justice, and to love
kindness,
and to walk humbly with your God? (Mic. 6:8).

Such potential dedication is carried over into the New
Testament.

> . . . [Be] doers of the word, and not merely hearers who deceive
> themselves. For if any are hearers of the word and not doers, they
> are like those who look at themselves in a mirror; for they look at
> themselves and, on going away, immediately forget what they were
> like. But those who look into the perfect law, the law of liberty,
> and persevere, being not hearers who forget but doers who act – they
> will be blessed in their doings.

> What good is it, my brothers and sisters, if you say you have faith
> but do not have works? Can faith save you? If a brother or sister is
> naked and lacks daily food, and one of you says to them, Go in
> peace; keep warm and eat your fill, and yet you do not supply their
> bodily needs, what is the good of that? So faith by itself, if it has
> no works, is dead (James 1:22-25; 2:14-17).

> If I speak in the tongues of mortals and of angels, but do not have
> love, I am a noisy gong or a clanging cymbal. And if I have
> prophetic powers, and understand all mysteries and all knowledge,
> and if I have all faith, so as to remove mountains, but do not have
> love, I am nothing . . . . [Faith], hope, and love abide, these three;
> and the greatest of these is love (1 Cor. 13:1-2, 13).

As friends of God "doers of the word" unlock their lives to God's
friendship. In addition, will not responsible moral policy and action
help other human beings to meet and know God as Friend rather
than, or at least more than, as Enemy? However, no human ethic is
beyond criticism or exempt from moral evaluation – not excluding this
or that kind of Christian ethic. Thus, while Christianity's depth
and richness are made possible by its having "endured over a long
period of time, addressing itself to a variety of situations,
experiences, philosophies and cultures," it is Christianity's very
institutional authority that "gives continuity to its misogyny and

patriarchy."[3] There is continuing need for the ethicizing of any and every ethic.

———

The universe of Christian ethics is enormous and complex; the treatment that follows comprises but a partial glimpse of that universe. There is great agreement within the Christian community upon issues of morality – and there is great disagreement.

The Christian church is obligated to think through the moral task and to apply Christian principles to that task. In this regard, Christian ethics may and will fashion a threefold structure of *love-justice-power:*

First: The discrete *motivation* of that ethic consists in *love* for God, humankind, and the natural world, in response to God the Creator's and Redeemer's love for Christians in Jesus Christ.

Second: The experiential thrust and content of the issues dealt with by the Christian ethic – in collaboration with extra-Christian and extra-religious parties – have to do perforce with *justice* for human beings, extending as well to a responsible relationship to the natural environment.

Third: The morally indispensable instrument for the advance of justice is *empowerment.* Failing to provide and implement power, the programs and counsel of justice, while attractive, remain largely futile; failing to provide and implement justice, Christian love, while appealing, remains largely helpless.

The above three dimensions or phases of Christian ethics are developed in, respectively, the two following sections of this chapter (upon the people of Christ and the motivation of responding love; and upon the mending of the world), and in the first section of the next chapter (upon empowerment as *sine qua non*).

The People of Christ and the
Motivation of Responding Love

We here emphasize the *motivation* of Christian ethics.

The mainspring of a distinctively Christian moral praxis is gratefulness to God for God's merciful gift of Jesus Christ, God's free grace in justifying those who are ungodly (Rom. 4:5). The First Epistle of John moves from the universal consideration that all who love are born of God, to the special revelation of God's love in the

———

[3]Wendy Farley, *Tragic Vision and Divine Compassion* (Louisville: Westminster/John Knox Press, 1990), p. 33.

Incarnation, and thence to the unique motivation of Christian love: response to God's love.

> Beloved, let us love one another, because love is from God; everyone who loves is born of God and knows God. Whoever does not love does not know God, for God is love. God's love was revealed among us in this way: God sent his only Son into the world so that we might live through him. In this is love, not that we loved God but that he loved us and sent his Son to be the atoning sacrifice for our sins. Beloved, since God loved us so much, we also ought to love one another. No one has ever seen God; if we love one another, God lives in us, and his love is perfected in us. . . . We love because he first loved us (I John 4:7-12, 19).

As we have declared, the engine of the Christian life is obedient response to what God is and does.[4] This teaching has its origins in Judaism: "As the All-Present is called compassionate and gracious, so be you also compassionate and gracious."[5] Because God loves, Christians seek to love. Because God is just and covets justice, Christians seek to serve justice. Because God is righteous, Christians seek to uphold righteousness. Because God the Friend is faithful to God's promises, Christians seek to be faithful to their own promises. Because God is essentially a doing God, Christians seek to be doing people.

> Woe to him who builds his
> > house by unrighteousness,
> > and his upper rooms by
> > > injustice;
> who makes his neighbors work
> > for nothing;
> and does not give them their
> > wages;
> who says, "I will build myself a
> > spacious house

---

[4]A distinction is often drawn between an *agathological (teleological) ethic,* an ethic of consequences that seeks to realize "the good," and a *deontological ethic,* an ethic of duty that seeks to honor what is "right" apart from consequences (see A. Roy Eckardt, *For Righteousness' Sake* [Bloomington: Indiana University Press, 1987], pp. 8-9). In his counsel, "you need not hope to undertake, and you need not succeed to persevere," William of Orange typifies a deontological ethic in contrast to an agathological ethic. In an ethic of obedient response, agathological and deontological elements alike vie for a place.
[5]Mekhilta 37a, Shabbat 133b, cited in David Birnbaum, *God and Evil* (Hoboken: Ktav Publishing Company, 1989), p. 47.

with large upper rooms,"
and who cuts out windows for it,
    paneling it with cedar,
        and painting it with vermillion.
Are you a king
    because you compete in cedar?
Did not your father . . . do
    justice and righteousness?
        Then it was well with him.
He judged the cause of the poor
        and needy;
    then it was well.
Is this not to know me?
    says the Lord (Jer. 22:15-16).

For the Lord is righteous;
he loves righteous deeds;
    the upright shall behold his
        face (Ps. 11:7).

Hester Panim here holds itself in abeyance, if only for a time.

To Mend the World

We here stress the dimension of *justice*.

As stated above, the special motivation of Christian ethics is uniquely Christian, but the experiential thrust and content of the human problems dealt with by that ethic are shared publicly with the extra-Christian world – for the sake and to the end of justice. Christian ethics as such develops from within the Christian community of faith and is driven and maintained by uniquely Christian resources. However, the moral issues and challenges to which the church devotes itself are open to a "common front." It is not that our broken world can be made perfect by human effort. The deceptions of utopianism are to be avoided. Nevertheless, our world may be fashioned into a place where there is greater and greater justice for the disadvantaged and the suffering, and greater responsibility for the natural creation. The evils that are associated with human sin can be meliorated in indeterminate measure. "It is not for you to finish the task, but neither are you free to desist from it altogether."[6]

---

[6]Avot 2.16, as cited in Judith Plaskow, *Standing Again at Sinai* (San Francisco: Harper & Row, 1990). p. 238.

A Midrash asks why the Divine covenant with Abraham was required. "This," is the answer, "may be compared to a house on fire. People ask, Does the house have no owner? Through the children of Abraham God says, 'I am the owner of the house.'"

A Jew today still willing to convey this message has a question of his own: If the house has an owner, why does He not put the fire out? Perhaps He can and yet will. Perhaps He cannot or will not. But if He cannot or will not, a Jew today must do what he can to put the fire out himself.[7]

The same holds for the Christian.

Some two millennia ago, a number of rabbis came together in conference to debate a single issue: Should humans have been created or not? They debated and then took a surprising vote: No, by majority vote. We should not have been created since we appear to be incorrigibly evil. But because we have, they added, let us assiduously examine our ways, our lives so that we won't self-destruct and destroy everything with us. Let us engage relentlessly in *tikkun olam:* repairing and mending our world.[8]

The teaching of *tikkun olam* is originatively Hebraic.[9] From a Judaic perspective, humankind is the (grudging? willing?) partner of God in the implementing of justice upon the earth and in governing the world.

"Ye are My witnesses, saith the Lord, and I am God" (Isaiah 43:12). That is, when you are my witnesses, I am God, and when you are not My witnesses, I am, as it were, not God.

Genesis 1:26 states: "And God said: 'Let us make man in Our image . . .'" The Zohar responds to the question of why the plural "us" by explaining that man is a partner *(shutaf)* with the Divine in the creation of man. The rabbinic/kabbalistic concept of *tikkun olam* . . . further complements the theme of man's partnership with the Divine.[10]

Eliezer Berkovits writes that man "has been placed on earth that he may sanctify the secular, *l'taken olam b'malkut Shaddai,* and establish the city of man as the Kingdom of God. It is not either God

---

[7]Emil L. Fackenheim, *What Is Judaism?* (New York: Summit Books, 1987), p. 292.

[8]Editorial by Jack D. Spiro, *Religious Education* (1990): 330.

[9]Cf. Emil L. Fackenheim, *To Mend the World* (New York: Schocken Books, 1989). See also Plaskow, *Standing Again at Sinai,* chap. 6, "Feminist Judaism and Repair of the World." On Jewish ethics as such, consult the special number of *Shofar* on that subject: Vol. 9, No. 1 (Fall 1990).

[10]The first part of this dual citation is from Midrash Rabbah, Psalms 123:1; both passages appear in Birnbaum, *God and Evil,* p. 74. The Zohar is a work of kabbalistic mysticism, the main part of which comes from the late 13th century.

or man. Man, according to his own strength, continues the work of creation and becomes . . . a humble associate of the Creator."[11]

Adherents of the Christian faith have inherited (grudgingly? willingly?) a similar understanding. How faithful are they going to be to that heritage?

The Jewish journal *Tikkun* is dedicated to a "critique of politics, culture, and society" – in ways not unlike *Christianity Today*, on the Christian side. With the latter journal, *Tikkun* is committed to a politics of compassion grounded in the certainty that to be authentically human is to be *in relationship* to other human beings:

> Tens of millions of people live lives in which their fundamental human capacities – for intellectual and aesthetic activity, for freedom and self-definition, for loving relationships and solidarity with others, for creativity and meaningful work – are systematically denied and stunted. The decreasing opportunities to use one's intelligence and creativity in the world of work, the breakdown of communities, the crisis in families, the secularization of daily life – all have led to a reality in which large numbers of Americans feel deep pain . . . . [No] matter how powerful our moral vision, unless we speak to the pain of daily life few of our words will be heard or taken seriously.[12]

That the above wording could just as readily appear in a Christian organ is exemplary of the common moral front that characterizes the quest for human justice and that is in turn bolstered by that quest.

Such universality of thought and effort is further understood and exemplified by means of the category of "middle axioms," a term originated some years ago by J. H. Oldham and popularized by John C. Bennett. A "middle axiom" is construed as "more concrete than a universal ethical principle and less specific than a program that includes legislation and political strategy."[13] This understanding ties in with our own threefold structure of love-justice-power:

- The *love* that responds obediently to God's love *(agape)* gives life to a "universal ethical principle."

- The thinking and praxis that foster *justice* range themselves somewhere between universal ethical principles and the discrete work of social and political empowerment and enforcement.

---

[11] Eliezer Berkovits, *Faith after the Holocaust* (New York: Ktav Publishing House, 1973), p. 60.
[12] "Compassion as Hardball Politics" (editorial), *Tikkun* 1, 2 (1986): 7, 8.
[13] John C. Bennett, *Christian Ethics and Social Policy* (New York: Charles Scribner's Sons, 1946), p. 77.

   • Action in behalf of social and political *empowerment* implies
   programs of "legislation and political strategy."

As a term equivalent to "middle axioms," I suggest *norms of policy
making*.[14] The following list of twelve such norms is meant to be
representative and illustrative but not exhaustive. Some vital areas
of moral responsibility are simply omitted from consideration (e.g.,
the very debatable issue of abortion[15]; health care[16]; addictiveness
and the drug traffic; and crime and punishment.[17] Some themes (e.g.,
women's liberation) are reserved for our later discussion under the
category of empowerment. Certain themes in the present section could
conceivably be placed under the latter category and vice versa.
Again, currently pertinent norms or axioms are not held to be binding
for all time but are highly relative to given historical periods and
given circumstances. They reflect the demands that love makes upon
and within particular generations.[18] Finally, the norms referred to
here are not meant to be above all controversy. In the formulating of
the norms I have done my best to be morally positive while trying at
the same time to avoid undue partisanship. It would not be fitting in
these pages to propagandize for this or that specific political or
economic program.

   1. A responsible social ethic will oppose the notion that
humankind's "spiritual" needs and values are to take precedence over
its "material" needs and values – a notion that has definite
implications for such diverse areas as economic life and sex.

   Such an unfortunate notion most often reflects an ideology that is
dominant amongst that minority of people in the world who are free
from worry concerning food, health, and other necessities of life. Most
of the world's human population is poor, exploited, unfree. It cannot
afford the luxury of separating "spirit" and "matter," or of elevating
the one over the other.

---

[14]In a source I cannot recover, John Courtney Murray identifies *policy* as "the
hand of reason set firmly upon events." It is "the meeting-place of the world
of power and the world of morality."

[15]Upon this issue, consult Eckardt, *Jews and Christians* (Bloomington: Indiana
University Press, 1986), pp. 117-118; John B. Cobb, Jr., *Matters of Life and Death*
(Louisville: Westminister/John Knox Press, 1991), chap. 3. Cobb determines
that the question of abortion has to be approached with sensitivity "to the
massive oppression women have suffered and continue to suffer" (p. 90).

[16]See, e.g., Paul T. Menzel, *Strong Medicine: The Ethical Rationing of Health
Care* (New York: Oxford University Press, 1991).

[17]See essay on this subject by A. Roy Eckardt in Harold H. Hart, ed.,
Punishment: For & Against (New York: Hart Publishing Company, 1971), pp.
164-189.

[18]Bennett, *Christian Ethics and Social Policy*, pp. 77, 107.

2. Individual persons – Christians, Jews, Muslims, secularists atheists, et al. – are each responsible for making their own decisions respecting the fundamental moral problems and catastrophes of our time, within the context and with the aid, yet often in criticism, of the collectivities to which they belong. These people are the ones who bear the burden of, and have the blessed opportunity to engage in, partisan (i.e., *committed*) political decision-making.

3. However, today's challenge to advance human equality is not confronted responsibly without coming to grips with the systemic question. For instance, Allan Boesak points out that the issue that counts is not whether Blacks are to be equal to whites, but whether Blacks wish to be equals within the whites' kind of system.[19] The struggle to implement racial and other forms of equality – in accordance with the teaching that all are children of God, bearers of the *imago dei* – cannot succeed so long as socio-economic structures that foster and even guarantee inequality are allowed to perpetuate themselves.

4. The relation of moral particularity and moral universality will always produce and sustain a certain degree of tension. On the one hand, there is "an interconnectedness of humanity that makes the freedom of one people dependent upon the liberation of all. No one can be free until all are set free." Yet on the other hand, the waging of particular battles can hardly be postponed until other battles have been won.[20] Responsible human beings, plagued by finite time and finite resources, are forced to opt for *this* cause rather than *that* cause.

5. Upon the vital issue of human sexuality and its expression, there is a move within the churches of today – hotly debated – to go beyond a rule-ethic toward an ethic of the "good," interpreted in terms of human dignity, self-realization, and "right-relatedness."

A recent case in point is the report, "Keeping Body and Soul Together: Sexuality, Spirituality, and Social Justice," presented in February 1991 by a task force, the Special Committee on Human Sexuality, the Presbyterian Church (U.S.A.). The report was offered as a study document to be utilized in the church over a two-year period, with a view to adoption by the General Assembly of recommendations generated by the latter time of study. In June 1991

---

[19] A. Roy Eckardt, *Black-Woman-Jew* (Bloomington: Indiana University Press, 1989), p. 184; Allan Boesak, *Farewell to Innocence* (Maryknoll, N.Y.: Orbis Books, 1977), pp. 150-151.

[20] Eckardt, *Black-Woman-Jew*, pp. 184-185. The quoted words are from James Cone, *A Black Theology of Liberation*, 2nd ed. (Maryknoll, N.Y.: Orbis Books, 1986), p. xix.

the General Assembly roundly rejected the report.[21] I do not refer to the document here with any purpose of taking sides with it but only because it exemplifies the attempt, right or wrong, to work toward an ethic of the "good."

In words of the chairperson of the Special Committee, John J. Carey, "the committee recognized that previous Presbyterian statements have virtually ignored the sexual needs of singles [over 30 percent of the Church's membership], older adults, those with disabilities, people in institutions, and gays and lesbians." The report sought "to offer a positive theology of sexuality," in contrast to "the generally negative assessment in the Christian tradition of the place of sexuality in human life," a redeeming theology "that keeps body and soul together and that encourages Christians to think in positive ways about sexuality as a good gift of God," within a broad "perspective of human wholeness and faithfulness." The ethical guidelines the document advocated included "mutuality, consent, bodily integrity and self-direction for every person, responsibility for our choices and actions, and fidelity in our relationships." To be rejected is "the notion that the legal status of marriage should be the sole legitimation for sexuality that is sacramental or grace-bearing."[22]

To cite the report itself:

> [At stake today] is a deep, often bitter conflict over the normative character of our sexual and social relationships. In other words, what is at issue are our ethical values and commitments to an inclusive, egalitarian ethic of common decency . . . . [The] church needs to be teaching and embodying in its own ministry a higher and more demanding sexual ethic than one which passes judgments on the basis of highly formalized, patriarchal sexual categories. Such categories fail to do justice to the integrity of our lives as sexual-spirited persons; they also fail to empower us for justice-love . . . .
>
> . . . Where there is justice-love, sexual expression has ethical integrity. That moral principle applies to single as well as to married persons, to gay, lesbian and bisexual persons as well as to heterosexual persons. The moral norm for Christians ought . . . [to be] justice-love. Rather than inquiring whether sexual activity is premarital, marital, or postmarital, we should be asking whether

---

[21] The report was published in two volumes, a 196-page majority report (11 members) and a 70-page minority report (5 members). For an account of the defeat of the report, see editorial correspondence by David Heim, "Sexual Congress: The Presbyterian Debate," *The Christian Century* 108 (1991): 643-644.
[22] John J. Carey, "Body and Soul: Presbyterians on Sexuality," *The Christian Century* 108 (1991): 517, 518.

the relation is responsible, the dynamics genuinely mutual, and the loving full of joyful caring . . . .[23]

But in a forceful critique of "Keeping Body and Soul Together," Gary L. Watts finds the ethic of the report to be "empty," devoid of any really positive and crucially needed guidance to a contemporary Christian position on human sexuality:

> . . . While any ethical system must allow for exceptional cases which can only be decided by appeal to foundational values, a realistic system must also offer practical and specific guidelines for everyday use . . . . How can we in good conscience suggest that our advice to singles and adolescents consists of statements like "Where there is justice-love, sexual expression has ethical integrity"?
>
> . . . What is sorely lacking is a practical explanation of how justice and love will be better preserved by this new perspective than by the traditional one . . . .
>
> "Keeping Body and Soul Together" offers no real ethic at all. It assumes that human beings of all ages are capable of making demanding decisions in a moral vacuum, guided only by the general themes of justice-love and right-relatedness. It implies that the current crisis in sexuality demonstrates that the church's traditional ethic is outmoded and wrong . . . . [ignoring] the fact that much in our present chaos has arisen in the wake of the practical abandonment of this traditional stance . . .
>
> . . . Justice and love are sound biblical values. But we are fallen people who always try [how about "often try"? – A.R.E.] to twist those values to suit our own ends . . . . In the present document, justice and love have become independent values, detached from scriptural direction, authoritative in their own right . . . .
>
> . . . A church which maintains its credibility by abandoning its creeds in order to accommodate itself to society is a church that will soon be indistinguishable from that society. The call of the church is not to make itself credible, but faithfully to maintain the gospel which has been entrusted to it . . . .[24]

---

[23] "Sexuality and Justice-Love," excerpted from "Keeping Body and Soul Together: Sexuality, Spirituality, and Social Justice," by the Special Committee on Human Sexuality of the Presbyterian Church (U.S.A.), *The Christian Century* 108 (1991): 519.

[24] Gary L. Watts, "An Empty Sexual Ethic," *The Christian Century* 108 (1991): 520, 521. Karen Lebacqz denies that such concepts as "justice-love" and "right-relation" are empty: They are meant to convey "that God demands nothing more nor less than justice and love intertwined, and that *any* human activity that does not exhibit both love and justice is wrong. This means that sex is not right just because it takes place inside a heterosexual marriage: violent sexuality, abusive sexuality, dishonest sexuality is wrong even when hidden within the confines of church-sanctioned marriage. This also means that sex is not wrong just because it takes place outside those confines. It is not the *form* that makes sex right or wrong, but the *content* – whether it is genuinely

The foregoing debate comes down to two conflicting anthropological interpretations: the contention that human beings can indeed achieve faithfulness, be responsible, and be grace-bearing; and the opposing contention that human sinfulness necessitates a quite different approach to problems of sexuality. Any reconciliation between John J. Carey and (the majority of) his committee and such critics as Gary L. Watts will require some kind of implemented balance between the *yetser tov* and the *yetser ra*. That balance is not here to be found.[25]

6. To turn to a quite different though not unrelated challenge: In the aftermath of the collapse of state Communism, the Christian critique of unbridled capitalism is being continued and reinforced.

In a recent encyclical, "Centesimus Annus" (2 May 1991), Pope John Paul II repeats the traditional Catholic finding of virtues within a free market economy. Nevertheless, he emphasizes that a great many people lack the means to "take their place in an effective and humanly dignified way within a productive system in which work is truly central. They have no possibility of acquiring the basic knowledge which would enable them to express their creativity and develop their potential. They have no way of entering the network of knowledge and intercommunications which would enable them to see their qualities appreciated and utilized. Thus, if not actually exploited, they are to a great extent marginalized . . . ."

Many other persons "live in situations in which the struggle for a bare minimum is uppermost . . . [and where] the rules of the earliest period of capitalism still flourish in conditions of 'ruthlessness.' . . . In other cases the land is still the central element in the economic process, but those who cultivate it are excluded from ownership and are reduced to a state of quasi-servitude."

Again, many human needs "find no place on the market." Neither can profitability be the sole indicator of a company's conditions. "The purpose of a business firm is not simply to make a profit, but is to be found in its very existence as a community of persons who . . . are endeavoring to satisfy their basic needs, and who form a particular group at the service of the whole of society." Market mechanisms always "carry the risk of an 'idolatry' of the market, an

---

loving, life-serving, and just" ("Sex: Justice in Church and Society," *Christianity and Crisis* 51 [1991]: 174).
[25] Further to human sexuality, consult Cobb, *Matters of Life and Death,* chap. 4, "The Right to Love." Cobb emphasizes two issues, premarital sexual intercourse and homosexuality.

idolatry which ignores the existence of goods which are not and cannot be mere commodities."

There persists, finally, the problem of human alienation. According to the pope,

> . . . [Even] if the Marxist analysis and its foundation of alienation are false, nevertheless alienation – and the loss of the authentic meaning of life – is a reality in Western societies too. This happens in consumerism, when people are ensnared in a web of false and superficial gratifications rather than being helped to experience their personhood in an authentic and concrete way . . . .

> Against [the phenomena of marginalization, exploitation, and alienation] the church strongly raises her voice. Vast multitudes are still living in conditions of great material and moral poverty. The collapse of the Communist system . . . certainly removes an obstacle to facing these problems in an appropriate and realistic way, but it is not enough to bring about their solution. Indeed, there is a risk that a radical capitalistic ideology could spread which refuses even to consider these problems, in the a priori belief that any attempt to solve them is doomed to failure, and which blindly entrusts their solution to the free development of market forces . . . .[26]

7. Still within the socio-economic domain, the argument is heard that there must be an intensified and transformed stewardship of capital. In the words of "A Postcommunist Manifesto" by Max L. Stackhouse and Dennis P. McCann,

> We must invest in . . . new equipment for robotic production, in the development of nonfossil fuels and biotechnology, and in the training of a highly skilled work force. Failure to capitalize means not only economic stagnation but environmental destruction, unemployment, wider hunger and further homelessness. The undercapitalization that results from policies directed against economic growth inevitably compounds social injustice . . . . [We] must recognize that working to serve people's needs in the marketplace may be a holy vocation. . . . Further, public theology must insist upon a regard for the larger social and natural environment. In these ways, the disciplined pursuit of profits within a responsible strategy of capitalization can be a modern form of stewardship . . . .[27]

---

[26] "Excerpts From the Pope's Encyclical: On Giving Capitalism a Human Face," *The New York Times*, 3 May 1991.

[27] Max L. Stackhouse and Dennis P. McCann, "A Postcommunist Manifesto: Public Theology After the Collapse of Socialism," *The Christian Century* 108 (1991): 46. These analysts speak of "public theology" as reasserting "the imperative of theological discourse in the midst of jurisprudence, politics, culture, technology, sociology, and . . . economics" ("Max Stackhouse and Dennis McCann Reply," *The Christian Century* 108 [1991]: 83).

In criticism of Stackhouse and McCann, Barbara Hilkert Andolsen observes that "stewardship is a less central virtue for employees who have less corporate power. More crucial for them is solidarity with other employees in an effort to create and to maintain a workplace where the dignity of all is respected."[28]

8. Stackhouse and McCann continue that the modern corporation is a highly mixed blessing – a unique occasion for human creativity and social obligation, yet also a breeding place for human sin.

On the one hand, "societies stagnate and people die for want of the ability to form corporations"; on the other hand, "corporations become idols . . . when we bend all politics to their service, when their distinctive modes of operation get confused with the ideals that must govern health care, education, and culture . . . . To the extent that corporations are successful, markets cannot be relied upon exclusively to control corporations. The voice of labor, the demands of government, the rule of law must also be developed."[29]

9. Stress is to be placed not alone upon the *duty* of human adults to work, but upon their *right* to work, quite free from such extraneous factors as gender, race, and certain physical handicaps. In this connection, national and local communities have a shared obligation to ensure full employment.[30] The dual norm of labor as right as well as duty is of direct bearing upon the scandal of homelessness that afflicts American society.

The Executive Council of the United Church of Christ has adopted a policy prohibiting "discriminatory behavior or harassment" against church employees on the basis of "HIV/AIDS diagnosis or disability," adding this to prohibitions against discrimination grounded in race, color, national origin, gender, age, disabilities, or sexual orientation. Noting that an individual with HIV or AIDS "poses no risk of infection to coworkers," the council rules out pre-employment testing for HIV and AIDS, insists that the employee's health matters be kept confidential, and stipulates that no applicant or employee carrying the HIV virus who is otherwise capable of doing the job can be discriminated against because of her or his illness.[31]

10. There must and can be "an end to world hunger and . . . a reorganization of the world's resources and productive capacities so

---

[28]Barbara Hilkert Andolsen, "Socialism and Moral Imagination," *The Christian Century* 108 (1991): 79-80.
[29]Stackhouse and McCann, "Postcommunist Manifesto," pp. 46-47.
[30]Bennett, *Christian Ethics and Social Policy*, pp. 80, 81.
[31]"UCC and AIDS," *The Christian Century* 108 (1991): 512.

that poverty can be eliminated both in the U.S. and everywhere else."[32]

11. An additional item in this incomplete rendering of norms of contemporary policy making is taken verbatim from the journal *Tikkun:*

> [Liberals] must abandon their put-down approach to people who are attracted to religion. . . . If we understand the legitimate attractiveness of a community that articulates a vision of compassion for its members, if we can see the real value in the ideal of being forgiven [why not the *fact* of being forgiven? – A.R.E.] that is ingredient both in Yom Kippur and in the experience of born-again Christianity then we can see the current religious revival not as a threat to rationality but as a response to real and legitimate needs that our society fails to satisfy. We may reasonably wish to convince the growing religious communities that their compassion should extend beyond the borders of their own participants, but the discussion will never be heard as long as liberal intellectuals project an air of fundamental disrespect to those who take religion seriously.[33]

12. Perhaps more than anything else, we require a responsible policy for earth and environment.

Charles F. Melchert shows how "among the sages of Israel there is a close and intensive relation between the created order and justice – between what we would call, today, harmony within the global ecological system and global human and historical justice . . . . The sages say things like 'consider the ant,' 'listen to the birds,' 'see the lilies,' and 'think about a mustard seed.'"[34]

Sallie McFague concentrates upon the major contemporary paradigm shift in theology over to the question of how we are to save the physical world from "deterioration and its species from extinction." The focus of liberation theology has widened immeasurably "to include, in addition to all oppressed human beings, all oppressed creatures as well as planet earth [itself] . . . . [The] fate of the oppressed and the fate of the earth are inextricably interrelated."

Upon this I would comment that the problematic future of the earth means that we all live on the edge of oppression and misery. A common front becomes at once selfish and otherregarding.

---

[32] Michael Lerner, "Tikkun: To Mend, Repair and Transform the World," founding editorial statement of *Tikkun,* 1, 1 (1986): 6.

[33] "Compassion as Hardball Politics," p. 9.

[34] Charles F. Melchert, "Creation and Justice Among the Sages," *Religious Education* 85 (1990): 369, 375.

McFague attests that "the planetary agenda of the 21st century" summons us "to move beyond nationalism, militarism, limitless economic growth, consumerism, uncontrollable population growth and ecological deterioration." The enemy is we ourselves –

> indifferent, selfish, shortsighted, xenophobic, anthropocentric, greedy human beings. [There must be] a renewed emphasis on sin as the cause of much of the planet's woes and an emphasis on a broad and profound repentance . . . . [Theology ought] to underscore and elaborate on the myriad ways that we presently and corporately have ruined and continue to ruin God's splendid creation – acts which we and no other creatures can knowingly commit. The present dire situation calls for radicalizing the Christian understanding of sin and evil . . . . If theologians were to accept this context and agenda of their work, they would see themselves in dialogue with all those in other areas and fields similarly engaged: those who feed the homeless and fight for animal rights[35]; the cosmologists who tell us of the common origins (and hence interrelatedness) of all forms of matter and life; economists who examine how we must change if the earth is to support its population; the legislators and judges who work to advance civil rights for those discriminated against in our society; the Greenham women who picket nuclear plants; and the women of northern India who literally "hug" trees to protect them from destruction . . .[36]

---

[35]See Eckardt, "Consider the Animals," epilogue to *For Righteousness' Sake,* pp. 326-328; Cobb, *Matters of Life and Death,* chap. 1, "The Right to Kill." Cobb writes that the topic of animals and their treatment "most clearly challenges the anthropocentrism that has dominated our ethics" (p. 9).

[36]Sallie McFague, "An Earthly Theological Agenda," *The Christian Century* 108 (1991): 12, 15. Consult also Gibson Winter, *Liberating Creation* (New York: Crossroad, 1981), especially chap. 4. One version of a position known as "deep ecology" is Paul Shepard, *Nature and Madness* (San Francisco: Sierra Club Books, 1982). On the meaning and critique of deep ecology, consult Cobb, *Matters of Life and Death,* pp. 24-31. See also *SIDIC* (Rome) 22, 3 (1989), special number on "The Integrity of Creation"; and *Word & World* 11 (Spring 1991), special number on "The Environment."

7

What, Then, Are These
Christians To Do?, Part II

This chapter continues the exposition of norms of policy making.

Empowerment as Sine Qua Non

We here engage the question of social and political *empowerment,* the implanting of power.

The list of theses that follows is not quite as long as that provided under "To Mend the World" in the previous chapter; many of the themes of that section have either direct or indirect bearing upon the power issue.

As indicated in chapter six, it would be out of accord with the purposes of this book for me to take sides in dogmatic fashion amongst the necessarily partisan political challenges and duties of the day. Instead, I now single out eight theses wherein norms of policy making spill over from the category of the service of justice into the more discrete category of empowerment. For all the overlapping of categories, the essential principle holds: Without empowerment, justice tends to stay dreamlike and stilted, just as without justice, love is kept from loving.

1. Lamentably, the notion that human suffering is morally "valuable" is often utilized ideologically to deny power to the people who most need it.

The influential liberation theology and praxis of today stands in severe judgment upon the traditional propensity of theodicy to find something of special virtue or redemption in suffering.

> What kind of God . . . would wish blacks, women, Jews, or anyone else to suffer for the sake of others? . . .

On liberationist grounds, the traditional religious endeavor to assign special moral and spiritual value to human suffering is garbage . . . To argue today that by going to the Cross, Jesus condemned human survivalism is to inflict the hypocrisies and pretensions of white-sexist-gentile power-possession upon human beings who are suffering. People who insist that suffering is either ennobling or a moral-spiritual requirement . . . are invited to practice this principle upon themselves and are advised not to inflict it upon those who live and die under the heel of victimizers.[1]

Barbara Andolsen adds a needed twist to the above judgment: "[Feminist] ethicists have questioned sacrifice as the heuristic key to Jesus' ministry. They caution that some sacrifices that women are expected to make for privileged men are self-destructive and hence immoral."[2]

2. The empowerment of females is a top priority within sociopolitical action.[3]

Foremost among the moral causes supported by the journal *Tikkun*, in application of its editorial policy, is the woman's movement. "The most exciting and important development in contemporary Judaism" is the movement for women's liberation; that movement means no less than "a transformation of what it means to be a human being."[4] Parallel declarations can be made within contemporary Christianity as well as within much secular ethical thinking and praxis. As Madonna Kolbenschlag foretells – rather optimistically, I am afraid – "women's experience will be the hermeneutic of the future."[5]

From a plethora of possible exemplifications of the continuing challenge to empower women, two contemporary states of affairs may be mentioned. Women in rural Africa produce more than 70 percent of that continent's food, this without any benefit of tractors, oxen, or even plows. "Back-breaking hand cultivation is a job that African

---

[1]A. Roy Eckardt, *Black-Woman-Jew* (Bloomington: Indiana University Press, 1989), pp. 189-190 (slightly emended).

[2]Barbara Hilkert Andolsen, "Socialism and Moral Imagination," *The Christian Century* 108 (1991): 79.

[3]On the woman's movement as a whole, consult Eckardt, *Black-Woman-Jew*, chaps.7-13. On Christian feminist thinking, consult Anne E. Carr, *Transforming Grace: Christian Tradition and Women's Experience* (San Francisco: Harper & Row, 1988); Rebecca S. Chopp, *The Power to Speak: Feminism, Language, God* (New York: Crossroad, 1989); and Daphne Hampson, *Theology and Feminism* (Oxford: Basil Blackwell, 1990). See also note 12 to chap. 1.

[4]Michael Lerner, "Tikkun: To Mend, Repair, and Transform the World," founding editorial statement of *Tikkun* 1, 1 (1986): 11.

[5]Madonna Kolbenschlag, "Abortion and Moral Consensus," *Christianity and Crisis* 102 (1985): 183.

men consider to be demeaning 'women's work.'" In the great majority of African lands, women cannot inherit or own land. Boys are encouraged to go to school, girls not. In many places, women treat wife-battering as an acceptable practice.[6]

In the United States, an American Association of University Women study of 3,000 children nationwide has found that, while at the age of nine most female children are self-confident, assertive, and feel positive about themselves, by the time they reach high school less than a third feel that way. Although self-esteem drops somewhat for boys, there is no comparison; boys in elementary school have a much higher sense of self-esteem than girls and they tend to retain it through the high school years.[7]

Lena Malmström of Uppsala, Sweden has prepared the following confession of sin, to be used by women:

> O Lord, I confess before you that I have not believed
>   in my own possibilities, but
> by thoughts, words and deeds I have belittled myself
>   and my capacities.
> I have not loved myself as much as others. I have not
>   loved my body, my looks,
> my gifts, my very own way of being.
> I have let others govern my life; I have allowed my-
>   self to be disregarded and
> abused.
> I have believed the judgments of others more than
>   my own.
> I have allowd people to be disrespectful and spite-
>   ful toward me without daring
> to tell them to stop and desist.
> I confess that I have not dared to aim at my full
>   potential. Cowardly, I have
> avoided a fight when my case was just. I have bowed
>   out in order to avoid
> trouble.

---

[6]Jane Parlez, "Uganda's Women: Children, Drudgery and Pain," *The New York Times*, 24 Feb. 1991.

[7]Suzanne Daley, "Little Girls Lose Their Self-Esteem On Way to Adolescence, Study Finds," *The New York Times*, 9 Jan. 1991. Significantly, many more black girls continue to be self-confident in high school compared to white and Hispanic girls. One hypothesis applicable here is that black girls are more often surrounded by strong women whom they admire.

I confess that I have not dared to be as capable as
I can be.
O God, father and creator,
O Jesus, brother and savior,
O Spirit, mother and comforter,
forgive me for despising myself.
Restore me, make me trust myself, give me the true
    love of self.[8]

The only thing that bothers me in this marvelous prayer is that it gives the impression once again of insinuating that women carry the culpability!

We may take note of the connection Rita M. Gross establishes between the obligation to reunify God and the obligation of *tikkun*. Gross refreshes our memory of the Kabbalah, which attests that

> *galut* – exile – is the fundamental reality and pain of present existence. [The Kabbalah] teaches that one of the causes of *galut* is the alienation of the masculine from the feminine in God, the alienation of God and the *Shekhinah* [the immanent Presence]. But it also teaches . . . that each of us can effect the turning of *galut* by dedicating all our efforts to the reunification of God and the *Shekhinah*. Now that the masculine and feminine have been torn asunder and the feminine dismembered and banished, both from the discourse about divinity and from the human community, such a *tikkun* is obligatory, is a *mitzvah* [blessed deed]. When the masculine and feminine aspects of God have been reunited and the female half of humanity has been returned from exile, we will begin to have our *tikkun*. The world will be repaired.[9]

3. The crime of rape is incomparable, demanding special structures of power (capital punishment for rapists? the arming of females?) to overcome or at least to reduce its increasing incidence.

Upon the occasion of the disclosure of a rape victim's name by *The New York Times* (after other media had done so), two of the letters to the newspaper were the following, the first by Daniel C. Silverman, a psychiatrist with many years experience in rape crisis intervention:

---

[8] Reproduced in Brita K. Stendahl, "Lutheran Women towards 2000," *Word & World* 11 (1991): 286.

[9] Rita M. Gross, "Steps toward Feminine Imagery of Deity in Jewish Theology," in Susannah Heschel, ed., *On Being a Jewish Feminist: A Reader* (New York: Schocken Books, 1983), p. 234. I think that the phrase "God and the *Shekhinah*" is unhappy; it implies that "God" is the male side of deity. Cf. Raphael Patai, *The Hebrew Goddess* (Hoboken: Ktav Publishing Company, 1967).

I am most concerned by the absence of any serious discussion of what may be in the best psychological or medical interests of any particular rape victim or of rape survivors in general.

In countless studies . . . we have learned of the marked under-reporting of rape and the significant delay and great trepidation with which . . . survivors seek professional medical, psychological and supportive assistance. The reasons for reticence are related to the guilt, degradation and powerlessness of an individual subjected to the overwhelming terror and loss of control in rape. Those who would decide for the survivor of rape whether or not to identify herself or himself run the risk of helping to repeat the devastating experience of loss of control over one's life and amplifying the feelings of exposure, shame and humiliation in every rape survivor . . . . If we have learned any lesson in the work of helping survivors of rape, sexual and physical abuse to recover, it is that they must control the therapeutic process in their fashion and according to their timetables . . . .

The painful, persistent aftermath experienced by survivors known as rape trauma syndrome . . . exacts a toll in symptoms of post-traumatic stress disorder, damaged capacity for intimacy and problems in psychosocial adjustment.

The other letter was from Pamela C. Johnston, Executive Director of Victims Information Bureau of Suffolk.

It is easy for powerful, male editors and broadcasters to rationalize that rape should be treated like any other crime . . . . But rape is not like any other crime.

While most victims of crime feel embarrassment and self-blame . . ., survivors of rape feel especially humiliated and traumatized. Rape is a crime of power, control, anger, leaving the victim feeling powerless and damaged. The rapist dehumanizes his victim, and the victim feels her or his most intimate self has been violated . . .

Until law enforcement, lawyers, juries and the public stop looking to the victim for the motive of the crime, rape victims will still feel stigmatized . . . [10]

4. Allan Boesak epitomizes the morality of human liberation as such: "To be truly human one must have power." The sober truth is that liberation does not come from the preaching of "middle axioms" of justice; it is created only through revolutionary political and economic action: the appropriating of power.

Whenever an oppressed grouping succeeds in abolishing the religious or theological glorification of powerlessness, it thereby fights off the menace of its own victimization. And whenever it is able to counteract the misuse of whatever power it has managed to gain, it lessens the danger of itself becoming a victimizer. Thus, both

---

[10] *The New York Times,* 7 May 1991.

normatively and phenomenologically construed, an ethic of power is seen to be heavily relational. Possessed power (empowerment) is a *sine qua non* of liberation, yet oppressors can and do use power for evil purposes. This means that power as such is neither good nor bad. Power can be utilized for weal or woe. Belonging as it does to "the very essence of humanity," power – like freedom – is contingent for its potential goodness and legitimacy upon what humanity does with it.[11]

An American officer was heard to comfort a small band of terrified Iraqi prisoners of war: "It's all right. It's all right." Power was here breaking through into justice, and justice into compassion.

5. Much liberative thinking/praxis of today deems political pacifism to be indefensible and "a guarantee and perpetuator of the oppression that violent, powerful people visit upon the helpless."[12]

Political pacifism involves the notion that "nonviolence" is the only really morally and justifiably effective weapon for confronting the violence and oppression that are engaged in by human collectivities – this in essential contrast to "vocational" or personal pacifism, including the witness of those peace groups that do not construe their pacifism as an instrument of political efficacy.

Overall, in Christian circles doctrinaire, or political-pragmatic, pacifism seems to perpetuate the church's religio-cultural inheritance of a dichotomy of "spirit," regarded as "good," and "matter" or "body," regarded as suspect (a dichotomy from which Judaism has for the most part been spared). Such pacifism appears to many oppressed people as "an ideological act of sin, propounded in the name of virtue." However, this objection does nothing to make political-military violence in itself redemptive, or any kind of substitute for the many available instruments of nonviolent social change. (Yet cf. Stalin's famous question: "How many divisions can the Pope put in the field?") Furthermore, we are confronted by the stubborn fact that

---

[11] Eckardt, *Black-Woman-Jew*, pp. 186-187; Allan Boesak, *Farewell to Innocence* (Maryknoll, N.Y.: Orbis Books, 1977), p. 79, interpreting the thought of Manas Buthelezi; Michael Berenbaum, "Women, Blacks, and Jews: Theologians of Survival," *Religion in Life* 45 (1976): 115; see also Boesak, pp. 47, 50, 52.

[12] The material under this fifth heading has been adapted from Eckardt, *Black-Woman-Jew*, pp. 187-188; quoted wording is from those pages. On the matter of violence/nonviolence, consult Salo W. Baron and George S. Wise, *Violence and Defense in the Jewish Experience* (Philadelphia: Jewish Publication Society of America, 1977); Reinhold Niebuhr, *Christianity and Power Politics* (New York: Charles Scribner's Sons, 1940). For a political-pacifist argument, see John H. Yoder, *The Politics of Jesus* (Grand Rapids: Eerdmans, 1972).

amidst the present "advanced" state of war-making, different parties can appeal to one and the same "just war" tradition of the church and come out with opposed conclusions. Such was the state of affairs during the United Nations-Iraq War of 1991.[13]

Again, in the so-called Gulf War there was overwhelming support by Americans of their country's pursuit of the war. But there was strong opposition among church bureaucracies, e.g., the National Council of Churches and certain denominational hierarchies. A lack of "higher" ecclesiastical influence upon church members is often noted. In this particular case, such a lack could either be lamented or applauded, depending upon one's position on the war.

A further complication in the perennial argument between pacifists and nonpacifists is today's feminist critique, which knows well the evil of male violence and the crying need for alternative political strategies and weapons. Do not warfare and its ideological supports reflect and perpetuate age-old androcentric drives and hidden male destructiveness? Unfortunately, an affirmative reply to such questions is hardly of practical use to females in overcoming their own oppression. For the challenge continues to be "how to wrest power from the oppressing male. How can violent structures ever be collapsed without resort to violence?"

A practical complication *within* the foregoing complication is the increasing presence of women in American and other armed forces.

6. The method of human empowerment that most closely implements Jewish and Christian anthropology (the understanding of the nature and end of humankind) is political democracy, conceived as a method or system of power allocation.

In chapter 2 above, the biblical apprehension of what human beings are like is briefly sketched. We may here be reminded of Reinhold Niebuhr's aphorism, "Man's capacity for justice makes democracy possible; but man's inclination to injustice makes democracy necessary."[14] Democracy is a middle way between and beyond the extremes of political absolutism and political anarchy. The absolutist pretends that ordinary human beings are not fit to govern themselves; the anarchist fancies that there is no real need for humanity to be governed. But political absolutism means tyranny,

---

[13] A case in point was the employing of just war criteria by both James Turner Johnson and Alan Geyer respecting the UN-Iraqi War, the one analyst coming out in support of the war and the other rejecting it ("Just War Tradition and the War in the Gulf," *The Christian Century* 108 [1991]: 134-135).

[14] Reinhold Niebuhr, *The Children of Light and the Children of Darkness: A Vindication of Democracy and A Critique of Its Traditional Defence* (New York: Charles Scribner's Sons, 1946), p. xi.

and political anarchism means chaos. In truth – biblical Judaism and biblical Christianity alike imply – human beings are not so evil that they cannot achieve tolerable levels of justice and self-government (here enter the teachings of *yetser tov* and *imago dei*, the dignity of humankind), and human beings are not so good that they can be perforce counted upon to serve the commonweal (here enter the teachings of *yetser ra* and humankind as sinful, a self-serving idol-fashioner).

In the American system of constitutional checks and balances, found as well in some other countries, there is necessary recognition that human beings are not to be trusted, and equally full recognition that the very same human beings can be peculiarly trustworthy. The biblical teaching upon humankind escapes the twin maladies of utopianism and cynicism. The cynic may be identified as an idealist who has learned something. The Jew and the Christian, nurtured and sustained by biblical anthropology, are neither cynics nor idealists but realists, in politics as in everything else – or (since we are concerned with norms here) they ought to be. As Winston Churchill said, democracy is the worst system of government – save for all the others.[15]

Lord Acton's aphorism is often cited: Power corrupts; absolute power corrupts absolutely. This finding may be counterbalanced by another: Powerlessness corrupts; absolute powerlessness corrupts absolutely.

7. Mutuality of interest can be increasingly uncovered and encouraged between and among conflicting social and political entities.

A "zero-sum" moral condition refers to states where an advantage for one party must produce a disadvantage for another party. Zero-sum conditions may often be overcome. For example, efforts can be made to find and develop those points of mutual self-interest between Israeli Jews and Palestinian Arabs that may remove or reduce zero-sum conditions and make for peace and prosperity for both sides. "Is Cedric Mayson unexceptionally right that 'liberation is a prerequisite of reconciliation'? Must the reverse, 'reconciliation is a prerequisite of liberation,' be dismissed . . ., or is there not a grain of truth in that? May not liberation sometimes contain within itself the

---

[15]I do not maintain that the religious tradition we have inherited is necessarily pledged to political democracy as a moral norm. For centuries, the Christian church lived with, and even sanctioned, a nondemocratic political order. Along this same line, it is highly questionable whether the teachings of Islam can be utilized to provide a foundation for political democracy.

beginnings of human reconciliation? It does appear to me that there
is a bridge from human liberation to human reconciliation. The bridge
stands at the transition-point between zero-sum states and the
transcending of zero-sum by means of mutual interest."[16]

Although common fronts are not perforce easy to come by, some of
them are waiting to be consummated or at least built up. For instance,
Blacks and women are enabled to campaign as one for civil rights
enforcement.[17]

8. It remains essential that in the sphere of practical moral
action, love and justice be kept in dialectical tension. For the
selflessness of love sometimes serves to compromise and inhibit the
necessary reckonings of justice and the necessary operations of "power
politics." True, the prophet Jeremiah disallows any separation
among the divine love, justice, and righteousness. But we are not God.
And we are not Jesus Christ. When human political responsibility is
turned into perfectionism, it is no longer acting responsibly. Paul
Tillich's assertion that *justice* is "the true power of being"[18] may well
be kept in mind.

A caveat is thus required against any notion that the divine
kenosis is translatable univocally and unqualifiedly into human
morality. Jesus said that the second commandment is to love the
neighbor *as one loves oneself* (Mark 12:31). Self-love *accompanies* the
creative and enduring love of others; an unqualifiedly self-abnegating
ethic would menace the justice without which love is forced to stay
powerless. The ethic of love is to be balanced and indeed fulfilled by
the righteousness that is an everflowing stream (Amos 5:24).[19]

Sister/Brother Faiths

A separate heading is in order for what a Christian ethic may
have to say about the relation of the Christian faith to other
religions. This is a particularly salient moral issue, not alone in view
of the long history of Christian intolerance, supersessionism, and

---

[16]Eckardt, *Black-Woman-Jew*, pp. 186, 191 (slightly emended); in general,
chap. 17, "Beyond the Fate of Zero-Sum."

[17]*Ibid.*, p. 186. But Laura Anne Silverstein rightly reminds us that feminism
goes far "beyond the civil rights movement, and its success depends on its
ability to divorce itself from civil libertarianism when necessary." It is false
and even misogynist to reduce the women's movement to a subcategory of the
civil liberties movement (letter in *The New York Times,* 24 Nov. 1987).

[18]Paul Tillich, *The Socialist Decision,* trans. Franklin Sherman (New York:
Harper & Row, 1977), p. 6.

[19]A. Roy Eckardt, *Reclaiming the Jesus of History* (Minneapolis: Fortress Press,
1992), p. 203.

imperialism, but from the standpoint of vital human relationships in today's increasingly single world.

1. An overall typology upon the question of human truth and truth-claims may be worded as follows (without disallowing in-between positions or other possible refinements):

> *Absolutism.* "Our truth" is the only (saving) truth. (Sometimes known as exclusivism.)

> *Relativism.* There is no such thing as one truth. Various human truth-claims are in essence determined by limited, particular states of affairs and interests.

> *Relationism.* This view moves dialectically between absolutism and relativism. Human beings are capable of relating to and expressing some measure of authentic truth, although at best their truth-claims comprise fractional or incomplete glimpses or representations of truth.

Absolutism makes unqualified truth-claims; relativism makes no really objective truth-claims; relationism makes qualified truth-claims. From an extreme Christian absolutist perspective, Christianity is "true" and other religions are "false" (not excluding Judaism, which becomes especially subject to the "judgment" of "God in Christ"). From a relativist perspective, it makes no sense to go around pinning labels of "true" or "false" upon one or another faith. From a relationist perspective, it is quite licit to speak of Christianity as somehow participating in the truth of God, while not ruling out the presence and support of God within alternative faiths.

The third of these points of view opens the door to Christian allowance for socio-religious pluralism, not alone as a concession to human quarrelsomeness (though certainly that) but also as a logical embodiment of a certain way of construing religious truth. These days the third outlook seems to be of increasing influence, and it is, for better or worse, an assumption of this book. Once we affirm that God is involved in all of human creation and history, it follows that extra-Christian spirituality as such must somehow mirror the life and will of God. For it is simply loose reasoning, and hence a reasoning that does not convince, to argue that since Jesus Christ is (rightly) believed by Christians to be their Savior or Redeemer, therefore no other means of salvation or redemption is available for nonChristians. However, I agree with Paul F. Knitter that to bar the absolutist position from any and all possibility of correctness would be intellectually dishonest.[20] But the same holds, I should think, for the relativist outlook and, for that matter, the relationist claim.

2. Paul Knitter offers a version of relationism that merits serious attention. His favored phrase is "theocentric Christology."

Knitter, a Roman Catholic theologian, prefaces his constructive view with the question of what is *felt* by those who commit themselves to Jesus Christ. While these people surely experience that Christ is utterly reliable and demanding as an expression of who God is, and also that "Christ has something crucially important to say to all peoples (universal relevance)," Christian experience simply does not imply "that Christ is the *one and only* utterly reliable and demanding expression of God's reality. When a Christian experiences Jesus Christ to be 'my savior' and [even] 'savior for all,' that does not necessarily mean 'only savior.'"

Constructively speaking, Knitter shows how much contemporary Christology, Catholic and Protestant, is moving towards nonexclusivist or nonabsolutist interpretations of Jesus Christ. His own theocentric model is held to offer a "relational uniqueness, meaning a uniqueness that is able to relate to, to include, and to be included by, other unique religious figures." We stand today in need of a "renewal or return to the theocentrism that marked" Jesus' own understanding of his mission and of himself.[21] A theocentric theology of religions "need in no way diminish one's personal and full commitment to Jesus as incarnation of God's saving purpose and presence." On the contrary, this kind of understanding can well "confirm and intensify" the commitment to Jesus "by rendering it more intellectually coherent (better theory) and more practically demanding (better praxis)."

Knitter calls for a confessional Christian approach to others. Such an approach

> will be both certain and open-ended. It will enable Christians to take a firm position; but it will also require them to be open to and possibly learn from other positions. It will allow them to affirm the *uniqueness* and the universal significance of what God has done in Jesus; but at the same time it will require them to recognize and be challenged by the *uniqueness* and universal significance of what the divine mystery may have revealed through others. In boldly proclaiming that God has indeed been defined in Jesus, Christians will also humbly admit that God has not been confined to Jesus.[22]

---

[20] Paul F. Knitter, *No Other Name? A Critical Survey of Christian Attitudes Toward the World Religions* (Maryknoll, N.Y.: Orbis Books, 1985), p. 89.
[21] Jesus, who gives himself as a ransom for many (Mark 10:45), hardly bears out in his life the triumphalism within traditional Christian teaching. Must we not rather say that Jesus stands in judgment upon such triumphalism?
[22] Knitter, *No Other Name?*, pp. 142-143, 171-172, 181, 200, 203-204.

3. On the Protestant side Sharon H. Ringe gives voice to a point of view not unlike Knitter's. "How can we proclaim something as absolutely true without claiming it as also exclusively true? How can we retain the humility appropriate to our historical and cultural relativity, without allowing the proclamation of our faith to degenerate into a relativism that belies the fact that God's grace has met us in Jesus of Nazareth, whom we confess as Lord and Christ?" For Ringe, nonetheless, any claim that the new covenant in Christ renders others null and void constitutes "peculiarly unbiblical arrogance." Our challenge "is to hold to our *compromiso* (commitment) without compromise, but to find ways to do so in speech that does not exclude either other's experience or God's 'freedom' to speak in other voices with humankind."[23]

I may add a comment of relevance to Ringe's reference to the dilemma of absolutism and relativism. An effort to marry, or to allow at one and the same time for, the opposite or even seemingly contradictory attitudes to truth in absolutism and in relativism may not be as far-fetched as it first sounds. This may be seen via an example taken from mathematical theory. "Zenith" and "nadir" are expressible, respectively, as the end point of a straight line proceeding straight above an individual reality and the end point of a straight line proceeding straight below an individual reality. Theoretically, i.e., geometrically, the line in its "totality" proceeds into infinity in either or both directions. A more "absolute" line than this is not easy to think of. (Were the objection forthcoming that "space is curved," we should at most simply be met by an infinite circle, with zenith and nadir meeting at some absolute point.) Yet simultaneously, the blessed duality of zenith and nadir remains wholly (disappointingly?) relative to the individual and the individual's movements. Further, there are as many zeniths and nadirs as there are discrete entities: humans, animals, rocks, etc., etc. The absolute and the relative are here joined.

Upon parallel reasoning, we are met by such an oxymoron as "Religion X is the one truth; Religion X is not the one truth." It then stays incumbent upon the advocate of such an oxymoronish claim to convince us how it makes sense to propound such a statement. (A case comparable to such a claim is the synergistic reasoning that divine grace and human will are alike factorial to salvation [cf. Phil. 2:12].)

---

[23]Sharon H. Ringe, "Reflections on the Questions," in "God's Unbroken Covenant with the Jews," *New Conversations* (United Church of Christ Board for Homeland Ministries) 12, 3 (1990): 28-29.

4. It remains all-too evident that the foregoing rudimentary treatment of the problem of truth vis-à-vis sister/brother religions does nothing to settle the issue of how Christians are to reckon with nontheocentric and nontheistic faiths. However, I believe that the principle of relationism can be made to apply to these other encounters, even though we are not able to pursue the matter here.[24]

The Christian ethic of interfaith relations continues to challenge us as we ask in the chapter to come, Is there a Christian laughter? The two chapters of our closing Part III may help to reinforce the inseparability of Christian faith and Christian ethics.

---

[24]For additional studies dealing with Christianity and sister/brother faiths, consult D. Mackenzie Brown, *Ultimate Concern: Tillich in Dialogue* (New York: Harper Colophon Books, 1965), pp. 100-156; Arnulf Camps, *Partners in Dialogue: Christianity and Other World Religions,* trans. John Drury (Maryknoll, N.Y.: Orbis Books, 1983); Harvey Cox, *Many Mansions: A Christian's Encounter with Other Faiths* (Boston: Beacon Press, 1988); Gavin D'Costa, ed., *Christian Uniqueness Reconsidered: The Myth of a Pluralist Theology of Religions* (Maryknoll, N.Y.: Orbis Books, 1990); Mary Kelly, ed., *In Memoriam Charlotte Klein: Christology and Religious Pluralism* (London: Sisters of Sion, 1990); and Wilfred Cantwell Smith, *Towards a World Theology: Faith and the Comparative History of Religion* (Maryknoll, N.Y.: Orbis Books, 1981).

Part III

CHRISTIAN TEACHINGS:
COMEDY-TRAGEDY-BEYOND TRAGEDY

8

Is There A Christian Laughter?

Much is said in chapters six and seven upon what Christians are to do. Are they not also called upon to *laugh?* But what does that mean?

To be human is to laugh – and to weep. When Christians laugh, are they to laugh, can they laugh, as Christians?

Continuity, Discontinuity

Jews and Christians, sharing their earthlingness, also share certain elements of vision *(Anschauung)*. This gives us two immediate considerations from which to work.

1. Amongst various readings of the character of human laughter and humor, none is more influential or wise than the bonding of comedy with incongruity-paradox-surprise. Surprise when awakening to an existence we have no part in bringing about may induce laughter of a kind, as it may also induce tears. The mystery of comedy is deeper than any of the three phenomena I have just joined by hyphens, yet comedy gets its worldly nourishment from them all and most peculiarly from incongruity, its very own mistress. Christian laughter lives with other laughters in the measure that it participates in human incongruity. Of course, not all incongruity makes for comedy; much of it is hostage to tragedy. Overall, human comedy seeks out some form of meaning amidst the meaninglessness that imperils life.

2. We have earlier reminded ourselves of the ongoing foundations of Christian faith within Jewishness. The question of Christian laughter may accordingly be the same in kind as other living issues within the continued conversation of Jews and Christians, issues having to do with God, humankind, morality, politics, the future,

and so on. As maintained in chapter three, Christianness and Jewishness stand, generally speaking, in a double relation of continuity and discontinuity. Let us see how this relation may work out respecting the mischievous (= unreservedly serious) reaches of humor and comedy. (It is fruitless to seek out the unique quality of Christian laughter in and through such a figure as Jesus and his teachings, since it was wholly within a Jewish world that he lived and died.[1])

Perhaps we can point to what Christian laughter is and is not by alluding to what it is that makes Jewish laughter distinctive. With help from Mark Shechner and others, we may think of Jewish humor in the context of the American scene but without losing sight of Jewish history and tradition as a whole.[2]

As a means of apprehending the two worlds that go to produce Jewish comedy, Shechner introduces the paradoxical phrase, "ghetto cosmopolitanism," a condition that "arose out of the striking conjunctions of oppression and spirituality in the ghettos and *shtetls* of Ashkenazic Jewry." The ghetto cosmopolitan "combines a parochialism bred of poverty and confinement with a universal consciousness bred of study and intellectual ambition. In him, vulgarity and sensibility go hand in hand; his coarseness of manner is not inconsistent with a high degree of intellectual and aesthetic discrimination."

The two worlds in which these Jews dwelt, and which their descendants continue to preserve in varying guises, are the exalted (transcending) world of Jewish spirituality with its own language, Hebrew, and the lowly (immanent) world of ordinariness with its

---

[1]Cf. Elton Trueblood, *The Humor of Christ* (San Francisco: Harper & Row, 1964). Trueblood points out that the kind of humor found most widely in the Gospels is irony. The massive traditional effort to divide Jesus from "the Pharisees," exemplified in Trueblood, has been pretty much vanquished by recent New Testament scholarship; see, e.g., E. P. Sanders, *Jesus and Judaism* (Philadelphia: Fortress Press, 1985), pp. 276-281; and A. Roy Eckardt, *Reclaiming the Jesus of History* (Minneapolis: Fortress Press, 1992), *passim*.

[2]I argue that distinctiveness in *Sitting in the Earth and Laughing* (New Brunswick: Transaction, 1992), chap. 11, from which parts of this chapter are adapted and wherein I utilize Mark Shechner, "Comedy, Jewish," in Glenda Abramson, ed., *The Blackwell Companion to Jewish Culture* (Oxford: Basil Blackwell, 1989) and particularly the source listed in note 3 below. A point of departure for such a reading of (American) Jewish humor is the intriguing datum that while a mere 2.7 percent of the U.S. population is Jewish, some 80 percent of its comic figures, writers, et al. are Jewish. A much more comprehensive analysis of Christian comedy is found in my study *How To Tell God From the Devil: On the Way to Comedy*, especially chap. 8 (forthcoming).

own language, Yiddish. Shechner observes that "a mind nurtured upon a higher and a lower language" is "accustomed to shuttling between the transcendent and the worldly and defining its relationship to reality in terms of the ironies generated by such travel."[3]

Instances of humor that live upon the unique incongruities generated by the two worlds of Jewry are legion. Mrs. Fishbein answers the telephone to hear a cultured voice, "Can you and your husband come to a tea for Lady Windermere?" Mrs. Fishbein cuts in, "Oy, have *you* got a wrong number!" Dahn Ben-Amotz asks, What if the people of Israel hadn't been elected the Chosen People?, and answers, "Some other people would have got it in the neck." An elderly Jewish lady art collector is apprised of a chance to secure another Picasso. She responds: "With Picassos I'm up to my ass already." And Woody Allen can agree that there is an intelligence to the universe all right – save for "certain parts of New Jersey." As Shechner writes, it was indeed the "juxtaposition of higher and lower worlds within the mental economy of the Jewish people that established the terms for a *comedy of deflation*, whose basic trope was a sudden thrusting downward from the exalted to the workaday. From Sholom Aleichem to Woody Allen, this comedy of internal juxtaposition has been fundamental."[4]

Much more would have to be said to authenticate fully, and to deal with objections respecting the above reading of, the special character of Jewish humor. But our concern instead is with Christian humor in continuity and discontinuity with Jewish humor. We have already distinguished between Jews as a *laos*, a people that sustains a particular faith but also runs beyond that faith, and Christians as in essence a community of faith. The reality of particular Jews *may* mean adherence to and observance of Judaism, yet it need not always do so; by contrast, the reality of Christians retains faith as its *sine qua non*. Jewish humor can be the humor of a people as such, and thus need not be "religious" (though, of course, one of its "worlds" is "spiritual"). Christian humor – if there *is* such a thing – is tied to Christian faith: no faith, no humor.

---

[3]Mark Shechner, "Dear Mr. Einstein: Jewish Comedy and the Contradictions of Culture," in Sarah Blacher Cohen, ed., *Jewish Wry: Essays on Jewish Humor* (Bloomington: Indiana University Press, 1989), pp. 142-146.
[4]Shechner, "Comedy, Jewish" (italics added).

Incongruity and the Christian Faith

Mark Shechner shows the relation of integral Jewish comedy to the religion of Judaism: "It is its inversion, its negative, its shadow. The reversal of figure and ground. Where both comedy and religion acknowledge the interdependence of two worlds, a higher and a lower, each gives primacy to a different world. Religion . . . translates upwards, while comedy undercuts the transcendent, criticizes it, subordinates it to the common. The one, in effect, Hebraizes, the other Yiddishizes."[5]

We are faced with a forbidding choice. It is entirely possible to fit Shechner's words sternly and exactly to the Christian situation, and conclude that there just is no such thing as Christian comedy. Or with Shechner's exposition as our point of departure, and holding on for dear life to the bond of incongruity and humor, we may be enabled to lift out the "subordination of the transcendent to the common" and utilize it to confess that Christian faith is itself a Joke: God hides Godself in *this* baby (John 1:14; 3:16) – not unlike the Joke that God hides Godself in Torah, the holy in the ordinary, the *kenosis* (emptying) of Eternity (cf. the Zen doctrine of *Sunyata,* emptiness).[6] What creates the *Joke,* as against just one more *joke* – the entire Christian story can be told by alternating lower-case words with words that boast capital letters – is a Realized Incongruity, a historical Event that dares to sustain within itself an entire Biology of human salvation.

As a matter of fact, the Christian church has been charged with the propagating of Three Jokes [Incongruities]: Christmas, Good Friday, and Easter. The other Jokes are: God died here, in this Jewish man (Matt. 27:50). And God raised this same person from the dead – what Paul construed as the foolishness of God at work (1 Cor. 1:25).[7] To resort to phrasing from today's humor studies, these are not

---

[5]Shechner, "Dear Mr. Einstein," pp. 154-155. Shechner ends his exposition by commenting upon the Irish comic tradition, which also arose out of a culture wherein religious authority was central to cultural formation. In both cases the comedy was aggressive and rude and struck with "antinomian force at the heart of the exalted" (p. 155).

[6]Consult John B. Cobb, Jr. and Christopher Ives, eds., *The Emptying God: A Buddhist-Jewish-Christian Conversation* (Maryknoll, N.Y.: Orbis Books, 1990).

[7]On a light note, and therefore perhaps an especially sober one, I once wrote: "What would be a better joke on those reactionary Sadducees than for God to raise her own Pharisee-liberal Son from the dead! She would be having a go at one of her dearest truths, and would be giving at least a few of her people a foretaste of the things that are to come. Maybe best of all, she would be reminding the Sadducees exactly what she thought of them, meanwhile

"funny ha-ha" jokes but "funny strange" or "funny peculiar" Jokes. Never conducive to guffaws, they rather arouse Awe (cf. "the numinous") and thence a Joyfulness of beauteous casts.

Yet how in the world could no less than *two* of the church's Three Jokes ever get legendized into, respectively, Santa Claus and the Easter Bunny? "Funny strange" was seduced by "funny ha-ha," or, differently put, the Awe/Joy of faith was convoluted into the entertainment of small (and large) children. (In our world, Entertainment has become king: Enjoy! Enjoy!) Is Realized Incongruity too dazzling for earthlings to endure? Perhaps the one Hope, speaking ecclesiologically, is that we have not succeeded, not yet anyway, in legendizing Good Friday. A .333 batting average is still pretty formidable. Furthermore, it is very good sometimes to have Scripture sound a warning against us: "He called a child, whom he put among them, and said, 'Truly I tell you, unless you change and become like children, you will never enter the kingdom of heaven'" (Matt. 18:3). From this point of view, William H. Willimon puts it all together: "At the heart of the Good News . . . is a God who throws caution to the winds and extravagantly, effusively, with a recklessness that can only be called comic, reaches out to us." More exactly, at Duke University "we do [Easter] for no better purpose than the sheer fun of it."[8] As in little children, the meaning of Joy *is* Joy, "a breath of childhood" (Gérard Bessière). In Santa Claus and the Easter Bunny we have conceded that the Terrible is there all right, too terrible to manage. The question remains: Who gets the last laugh?

Out of its *continuity* with Jewishness, the Christian church has somehow been enabled to keep viable the higher and lower worlds that comprise the dialectic of Jewish comedy (and apart from any linguistic duality). But out of its *discontinuity* with Jewishness, the church, while fully attesting to *some* kind of comedy of deflation, has yet altered the juxtaposition into a *translation downwards*, not undercutting the transcendent but transforming it.

Thus is Frederick Buechner empowered to tell of his conversion amidst a sermon by George Buttrick in a New York City church:

> [Buttrick] said that unlike Elizabeth's coronation in [Westminster] Abbey, this coronation of Jesus in the believer's heart took place

---

assuring her good friends the Pharisees that she was on their side" (A. Roy Eckardt, *For Righteousness' Sake* [Bloomington: Indiana University Press, 1987], p. 310).

[8]William H. Willimon, compiler, *Last Laugh* (Nashville: Abingdon Press, 1991), pp. 15, 16.

among confession – and I thought, yes, yes, confession – and tears he said – and I thought tears, yes, perfectly plausible that the coronation of Jesus in the believing heart should take place among confession and tears. And then with his head bobbing up and down so that his glasses glittered, he said in an old odd, sandy voice, the voice of an old nurse,·that the coronation of Jesus took place among confusion and tears and then, as God was and is my witness, great laughter, he said. Jesus is crowned among confession and tears and great laughter, and at the phrase great laughter, for reasons that I have never satisfactorily understood, the great wall of China crumbled and Atlantis rose up out of the sea, and on Madison Avenue at 73rd Street, tears leapt from my eyes as though I had been struck across the face.[9]

For David Heim, the Christian church "is, one might say, inherently comic, for it makes divine and universal claims in very human and particular ways."[10] But does not that make the Christian God inherently comic as well, for God too carries on in "human and particular ways"?

We are brought, then, to this life-and-death state of affairs:

	Form of Comedy	Source	
FOUNDATION ↑	Christian laughter	Transcendence transformed (Realized Incongruity)	↑ **FOUNDATION**
	Jewish laughter	The comedy of deflation	
	Laughter as such	Incongruity (Ground of humor)	

While the meaning and place of human laughter as such can be apprehended under the heading of incongruity-as-incongruity, and while the meaning and place of Jewish laughter can be grappled with intelligibly under the heading of the Jewish *laos*, there is no way to cope with the dimension of univocally Christian laughter apart from the concretions of Christian faith: Incarnation/

---

[9]Frederick Buechner, *The Alphabet of Grace* (New York: Seabury Press, 1970), pp. 43-44. This passage appears as the epigraph of Willimon, *Last Laugh.*
[10]David Heim, "Garrison Keillor and Culture Protestantism," *The Christian Century* 104 (1987): 518.

Crucifixion/Resurrection.[11] However, to be embraced by the Incarnation/Death/Resurrection of Jesus as special realizations of the promises that God has made to be present in the world is to stay entirely within the Hebraic province – as well as, I should dare to say, within the compellingly, liberatingly feminist province. The Resurrection (of this Jewish person) embodies and vindicates afresh the Jewish life-struggle against Necessity. In the name of human freedom and (anti-sexist) dignity and an open future, the revolution contra Fate *(moira)* moves forward and outward. The struggle is successively – not supersessionistically – joined by the Christian community of faith. Tragedy is countervailed by Comedy – by "confession and tears and great laughter."

If, as we declared in chapter 5, it is in the hiding that the love of God is given (the witness of Israel), and if it is in the giving that the love of God is hidden (the witness of the church), the dialectic of equality that we are granted between Jewishness and Christianness lives on and on: The laughter and the joy that erupt from both sides do not have to be triumphalist or arrogant. Rather are they together blossoms of grace.

A Plague on Superstition

For completeness' sake, one other query of an ancillary sort may be treated. Is there such a thing as a "Christian joke" (or a "Jewish joke")?

Many "Jewish jokes" are devoid of Jewish content, yet we receive them as instances of the Jewish dialectic of heaven and earth. All we need interject is that many such jokes simply reflect the cultural-historical background, ethos, or *Anschauung* of the Jewish people. It is probably the case that the formal identity and perhaps even the specific content of humankind's jokes are universal rather than being the property or invention of one or another people. If human laughter is itself a universal – grounded in incongruity – its creations ought to

---

[11] Cf. Paul Tillich: "The 'Cross of the Christ' and the 'Resurrection of the Christ' are interdependent symbols; they cannot be separated without losing their meaning. The Cross of the Christ is the Cross of the one who has conquered the death of existential estrangement. Otherwise it would only be one more tragic event (which it *also* is) in the long history of the tragedy of man. And the Resurrection of the Christ is the Resurrection of the one who, as the Christ, subjected himself to the death of existential estrangement. Otherwise it would be only one more questionable miracle story (which it also is in the records)" (*Systematic Theology*, vol. 2 [Chicago: University of Chicago Press, 1957], p. 153). The "Birth of the Christ" fills out the trialectic.

be universally available. But it has not been my purpose to wander out into the abstractions of universality.

Similar reasoning may apply in the instance of "Christian jokes." Christianity rests upon the Incongruity of Time as astonishingly "invaded" by Eternity. Certain apocryphal stories of the young carpenter Jesus have him magically stretching planks to a more workable size, or blowing into the mouths of clay birds to make them fly away. But to alter the blessed incongruities of the Christian faith into things ludicrous would be to reduce "funny strange" to "funny ha-ha." At a magic show everybody laughs. To change Incongruity into something wrongheadedly incongruous is to forget that the Incongruity of faith ever transcends superstition – as it transcends all mechanical manipulation.

So the question of whether there are "Christian jokes" or "Jewish jokes" is not really the point. Instead, Rabbi Lionel Blue of London can declare that "the most typical weapon of Jewish spirituality is humor."[12] From the standpoint of the present midrash, Christians may offer comparable testimony: The special weapon of Christian spirituality is a Joke.

In the end, the enigma of the nature, meaning, and human pertinence of Christianity is lived with in and through our answer to the question, Is there a peculiarly Christian laughter?

---

[12] Lionel Blue, *To Heaven With Scribes and Pharisees* (New York: Oxford University Press, 1976), p. 75.

9

The End and the Ending

> The God who brings to birth and destroys, gives forth and takes away, judges my limitations and calls me to struggle, is terrifying not for God's distance, but precisely for God's nearness.
>
> – Judith Plaskow

In this small book we have paused to reflect upon

- the deep of human sin and the height of human goodness (humankind's self-deification but humankind's self-transcendence);

- the wondrous but fateful datum of our "thrownness" into the world of (God's) creation;

- the testimony and the persistence of Christian faith amongst a congeries of human options;

- the Christian community as resting upon Israel, through which as through Jesus Christ membership is made possible within the people/s of God;

- the inevitabilities and fortunes of human faith (and faithlessness) and faith's concretion in Christianity;

- the wondrous tale of God's transfiguration from Void to Enemy to Friend, from an "It" to a "Thou";

- a God and a humanity that are called to share the *one* standard of righteousness;

- the life-struggle of God as Person, the One whose war against Evil is waged, not by thinking but by deeds of *teshuvah,* of compassion, of humility, a God whom Christians may forgive, a God whom Christians know as One-In-Three;

- the life-struggle of Christians to be a morally responsible community, pledged by its gratitude to God to join with others in the mending of a torn world through human justice and human empowerment;

- the solidarity of Christians with sisters and brothers of other faiths;

- and the odd sounds of Christian laughter in mischievous, haunting rivalry with the Hiding of God's face.

I grope for a summary phrase to describe whatever may have made sense in our little story. Perhaps "amazing grace" is the most adequate phrase. Rebecca S. Chopp attests that "grace is solidarity to live differently."[1]

Along the Rim of Despair

The one trouble is that the beginning of any new life is all too soon cut down by death.[2] This final chapter marks the principal end of the book, yet the extinction sure to be visited upon us all is the ending of every book, as of everything else. What is the point of Christian or any other forms of human assertion when, as John Maynard Keynes once put it, "In the long run we shall all be dead"? To identify God as "the principle of hope," which encompasses "the future of history,"[3] is of little comfort before the portent of history's funeral.

Chapter 8 concludes upon an upbeat note. But what is left once Christian laughter comes to its end? For C. S. Lewis, evil in general is characterized by lack of a sense of humor.[4] For Friedrich Nietzsche, "the devil is the spirit of gravity." From this point of view, it would appear that evil conspires with absolute gravity to win a very large battle: There is nothing funny about death. In the presence of death, comedy and humor are rendered helpless. In death, does not God our Enemy emerge as victor over God our Friend? If before the truth of death, sorrow must reign, how are we ever to repeat with John 16:22 that our hearts will one day rejoice, and that no one will take our joy from us?

---

[1]Rebecca S. Chopp, *The Power to Speak* (New York: Crossroad, 1989), p. 58.
[2]Consult the special number of *Religious Education* 85 (1990) on "The Pedagogy of Death."
[3]Michael Wyschogrod, *The Body of Faith* (San Francisco: Harper & Row, 1983), p. 168; in general, chap. 6. See also J. Christiaan Beker, *Suffering and Hope: The Biblical Vision and the Human Predicament* (Philadelphia: Fortress Press, 1987).
[4]W. Cary McMullen, "Villainy, Humor, and Heresy, *Theology Today* 46 (1989): 286.

To recast Christianity into a faith exclusively for this world and its responsibilities would be to concede that, ultimately speaking, Christianity is a failure, a futility, an untruth. For Christian faith would then have nothing to offer respecting life's central problem and life's central evil, the reality of death. "If secularity is a function of man having come of age, then death reminds him that coming of age is a prelude to the return to helplessness that waits at the end."[5] The paradox endures of what is to be done about death when, by awful definition, there is nothing, humanly speaking, that can be done about it. For in death, being gives every evidence of having been turned into nonbeing.

Perhaps the Second Vatican Council was right that humankind's bearing in itself "an eternal seed that cannot be reduced to sheer matter" accounts for the human rebellion against death.[6] Perhaps a person of perfect faith would neither fear death nor be exercised over their mortality. It would appear, however, that most people, conditioned by pride and beset with unbelief, scarcely look forward to their demise with equanimity.[7]

How, then, is it possible for Christians, sojourners with all humans "on the way to death," yet to claim that they are no longer aliens, no longer strangers to this world of things and other persons? (I hope I do not forget that my own yearning for life and more life only betrays my personal condition as a "fortunate" individual. Many people of our world would rather die than have to suffer as they do.)[8]

Hereafter, Thereafter

One way to grapple with the reality of death is to return to our Hebraic grounding and thence to our Christian inheritance.

---

[5]Wyschogrod, *Body of Faith,* p. 97.
[6]"Pastoral Constitution on the Church in the Modern World," 18, cited in *The Catechism of Modern Man (All in the Words of Vatican II and Related Documents)* (Boston: St. Paul Editions, 1968), p. 137.
[7]Reinhold Niebuhr, *The Nature and Destiny of Man,* vol. 1 (New York: Charles Scribner's Sons, 1941), p. 174.
[8]An indication that the value of life transcends a merely quantitative time-span is the yearning of a human being, amidst the absence of their beloved, the longing that the time pass quickly until the beloved is restored to them. Quite ready are they to wish part of their life away for the sake of such restoration! The human readiness and even wish to "kill time" reveal our transcendence of time – even though it is equally the case that time must finally kill us.

There comes to mind again the thought-provoking passage in the *Pirke Aboth,* one of the epigraphs of this book: The human being is not formed of its own will, does not die of its own will, and does not render of its own will the accounting it is to give to God. We have referred more than once to the first of these reckonings (God as potential Enemy?). We have questioned somewhat the second one. And here and now we enter upon the third. If the third reckoning is to convince, it must be treated as highly paradoxical, since the inevitability of any accounting before God would be at once meaningless and unjust apart from an insistence upon moral responsibility and freedom of the will. The central implication, however, is that the present life is not in fact the end but is succeeded by another. The perceptive reader will even ask: Could not the accounting humankind is to give to God – made licit only if there is human dignity and free decision-making – embody something of a *reparation* to human beings for having had no say in being born? And if we have not asked to be born, neither have we asked to be subjected to the specter of death. Someone other than us is the accountable party.

According to certain versions of religion, God "owes us nothing." Who are we to question God or to demand anything of God? The moral difficulty with this easy assumption has been intimated in chapter two. We bear no responsibility for having been created. This fact opens the door to a Christian affirmation that, since God is our creator, there is an authentic sense in which God does indeed owe us something. To be sure, we may, as moral beings, wish to show gratitude to God for our lives. Such a wish is basic within the Christian rationale for ethics. But the obligation is not all on the one side.

With the foregoing awareness of the human situation in mind, let us consider the biblical perspective upon death and the answer to death.

The human being, for all its self- and world-transcending capabilities, is "formed from the dust of the ground" and destined to return to that status.

> By the sweat of your face
> > you shall eat bread
> until you return to the ground,
> > for out of it you were taken;
> you are dust,
> > and to dust you shall return
>
> > > (Gen. 2:7, 3:19).

Once the spirit of God (Hebrew, *ruach;* cf. Greek, *pneuma*) is taken away, humankind is no more.

The Book of Job is categorical:

> But mortals die, and are laid
>> low;
>> humans expire, and where are
>>> they?
> As waters fail from a lake,
>> and a river wastes away and
>>> dries up,
> so mortals lie down and do not
>> rise again;
>> until the heavens are no more,
>>> they will not awake
>> or be roused out of their sleep
>
> (Job 14:10-12).[9]

The psalmist laments:

> You sweep them away; they are
>> like a dream,
>> like grass that is renewed in
>>> the morning;
>> in the morning it flourishes and
>>> is renewed;
>> in the evening it fades and
>>> withers . . . .
> For all our days pass away
>> under your wrath;
>> our years come to an end
>>> like a sigh.
> The days of our life are seventy
>> years,
>> or perhaps eighty, if we are
>>> strong;

---

[9]It is claimed of the writer of Job that he simply did not believe in an afterlife. But the end of the passage here cited may hint otherwise. And cf. Job 14:14: "If mortals die, will they live again? / All the days of my service I would wait / until my release [from Sheol] should come." On Job and the teaching of Sheol, see Job 3:17-19 and cf. Ps. 49:15: "God will ransom my soul from the power of Sheol, / for he will receive me."

even then their span is only toil
>   and trouble;
> they are soon gone, and we fly
>   away (Ps 90:5-6, 9-10).

The above form of lamentation is not absent from the New Testament. We read in the Book of James: "Come, now, you who say, 'Today or tomorrow we will go to such and such a town and spend a year there, doing business and making money.' Yet you do not even know what tomorrow will bring. What is your life? For you are a mist that appears for a little while and then vanishes" (James 4:13-14).

Nevertheless, from the biblical point of view the surety of death is matched by the surety of the world to come *(olam-ha-ba)*.[10]

A countervailing of the certainty of death is found in Ezekiel, prophet of the Babylonian Exile, who is brought "by the spirit of the Lord" and set down in a valley of bones. Ezekiel is told to prophesy that God will "cause breath to enter" the bones, will endow them with sinews, flesh, and skin, and they "shall live." "Thus says the Lord God: 'Behold, I will open your graves, and bring you up from your graves, . . . and I will bring you to the land of Israel'" (Ezek. 37: 1-12). Here the thisworldly dimension of Israel's resurrection will be noted. But the point is that the resurrection remains entirely the deed of God. Job's view that mortals "do not rise again" comes from the human side of things. Later tradition speaks otherwise, or better, speaks from the side of the grace and strength of God as Enemy of death.

During the period of the Second Temple, a developing feature of Hebraic eschatological ideas involved the linking together of universality, national hope, and individuality. At the "last day" God's judgment will be meted out to all peoples, not excepting Israel. From the second century B.C.E. the expectation of a final, universal judgment, apprehended in primarily collective terms, had become constituent to the Hebraic outlook. But the longings of the individual were given voice through the teaching of resurrection, which from rabbinic times onward became fundamental to Judaic doctrine. During the time of the Maccabees the prophet Daniel foresaw the awakening of the dead, "some to everlasting life, and some to shame

---

[10] It remains a highly moot question whether the *olam-ha-ba* is to be considered a transformed state of this space/time world or as blessedness that is "wholly other" *(The Encyclopedia of the Jewish Religion* [New York: Holt, Rinehart and Winston, 1965], pp. 289-290).

and everlasting contempt" (Dan. 12:2). The Pharisees believed in the teaching of resurrection; the Sadducees rejected it.[11]

Pharisee doctrine prevailed, as put forth in the second *b'racha* of the *Amidah:* "Thou sustainest the living with kindness, and revivest the dead with great mercy . . . Thou canst be trusted to revive the dead." Emil L. Fackenheim declares that it is clear why the rabbis came to affirm a world to come: "Given the belief in divine justice, the belief that justice is due to the individual, and the condition of this world, this affirmation is very nearly inevitable." The "righteous of all nations have a share in the world to come."

Fackenheim comments upon a paradoxical statement from the *Sayings of the Fathers:* "Better is one hour of *teshuvah* [repentance] and good deeds in this world than the whole life of the world to come; and better is one hour of bliss in the world to come than the whole life of this world" (*Abot* 4:22):

> Rabbi Jacob exalts [the one hour of *teshuvah* and good deeds] even in the sight of eternity, for it is unique. It is unique because each person is unique, and what makes him unique is the hour in which, as eternity holds its breath, he *makes himself* unique. The rabbinic world to come is not a case of escapism but its diametrical opposite. If anyone, guilty of escapism are those among the modern minded who dissolve human life into "Life," deny the uniqueness of each human life, and thus persuade themselves into denying the shock of the uniqueness of each human death. In contrast, the rabbinic affirmation of a world to come arises only on the grounds of a prior commitment, with Ezekiel, to the uniqueness of each person's life — and hence death in this world.[12]

---

[11] A. Roy Eckardt, "Death in the Judaic and Christian Traditions," in Arien Mack, ed., *Death in American Experience* (New York: Schocken Books, 1973), p. 134; S. G. F. Brandon, *The Judgment of the Dead* (New York: Charles Scribner's Sons, 1967), pp. 70, 71; Yehoshua Guttman and Menahem Stern, "From the Babylonian Exile to the Bar Kochba Revolt," in D. Ben-Gurion, ed., *The Jews in Their Land* (Garden City: Doubleday & Co., 1966), p. 154; *Encyclopedia of the Jewish Religion*, p. 331.

[12] Emil L. Fackenheim, *What Is Judaism?* (New York: Summit Books, 1987), pp. 270-272. W. B. Yeats asked: "Why do people think of eternity as a long long thing? It is the flash of light on a beetle's wing." I read Yeats's words in *In Praise of the Irish*, ed. Michael Downey (New York: Continuum, 1985), p. 22. Having been to Ireland, not once but twice, I venture the following testimony:

> To move
> From earth to heaven
> You will pass through Eire.
> Eire is the turnkey.

Yet what of the children of Auschwitz and all those victims in the *Shoah* who were murdered before they knew what was happening and hence could not or did not engage in the one hour of repentance and good deeds? (We do not forget such victims elsewhere and everywhere – A.R.E.) Fackenheim answers: "After this, is it possible to affirm the world to come? Over the years I have reached this conclusion: *Only if we share in the anguish of the victims dare we affirm their resurrection.* Only then dare we affirm the resurrection of anyone. For if the world to come does not exist for them, it does not exist at all."[13]

This brings us to the peculiarly Christian affirmation of resurrection and life after death, wherein both continuity and discontinuity with Judaism are to be found.

Reinhold Niebuhr stresses the biblical teaching of the "resurrection of the body" in contrast to the essentially Greek teaching of the "immortality of the soul" – though not "body" in a perishable sense.[14] Niebuhr does this as a means of pointing, on the one hand, to the unity of the human being as a creature of both nature and spirit (cf. above, chaps. 2, 3) and, on the other hand, to the quality of Christianity as a fully *historical* faith:

> The hope of the resurrection . . . embodies the very genius of the Christian idea of the historical. On the one hand it implies that eternity will fulfill and not annul the richness and variety which the temporal process has elaborated. On the other it implies that the condition of finiteness and freedom, which lies at the basis of historical existence, is a problem for which there is no solution by any human power. Only God can solve this problem . . . .
>
> In this answer of faith the meaningfulness of history is the more certainly affirmed because the consummation of history as a human possibility is denied. The resurrection is not a human possibility in the sense that immortality of the soul is thought to be so. All the plausible and implausible proofs for the immortality [everlastingness] of the soul are efforts on the part of the human mind to master and control the consummation of life. They all try to prove in one way or another that an eternal element in the nature of man is worthy and capable of survival beyond death. But every mystic or rational technique which seeks to extricate the eternal

---

[13] Fackenheim, *What Is Judaism?*, pp. 273-274.
[14] The Apostle Paul distinguishes between the perishable and weak body that is "sown" and the imperishable and glorious body that is raised (I Cor. 15:42-44); cf. Eckardt, "Death," pp. 127-128. For an intensive analysis of the conflictive elements in "immortality of the soul" versus "resurrection of the body," consult the latter source. With some exceptions, neither Judaism nor Christianity accepts the doctrines of transmigration of souls and the soul's reincarnation, views that are widespread within Eastern religious wisdom.

element tends to deny the meaningfulness of the historical unity of body and soul; and with it the meaningfulness of the whole historical process with its infinite elaborations of that unity . . . .

As against these conceptions of consummation in which man denies the significance of his life in history for the sake of affirming his ability to defy death by his own power, the Christian faith knows it to be impossible for man . . . to transcend the unity and tension between the natural and the eternal in human existence. Yet it affirms the eternal significance of this historical existence from the standpoint of faith in a God, who has the power to bring history to completion . . . .

Consummation is thus conceived not as absorption into the divine but as loving fellowship with God.[15]

The world to come is opened to humankind in a fully personal measure and a fully corporate measure. The teaching of resurrection allows equal places for human individuality and human social reality. Put to flight is the essential loneliness of the "immortal soul."

The First Fruits

The Christian persuasion of the hereafter attests to everything we have said concerning God and the grace of God as the sole answer to human powerlessness before the fact of death. Beyond this, however, the resurrection of Jesus Christ is interpreted as a kind of earnest of what is to come – not a guarantee in any wooden sense, much less a proof in any "scientific" sense, but yet a promise in a life-and-death sense. Thus in the Apostle Paul we encounter the paradox that the raising of the dead is a precondition of Jesus' resurrection, and yet that Jesus' resurrection serves to vindicate the precondition:

Now if Christ is proclaimed as raised from the dead, how can some of you say there is no resurrection of the dead [cf. the Sadducees – A.R.E.]? If there is no resurrection of the dead, then Christ has not been raised; and if Christ has not been raised, then our proclamation has been in vain and your faith [the Corinthians'] has been in vain. We are even found to be misrepresenting God, because we testified of God that he raised Christ – whom he did not raise if it is true that the dead are not raised. For if the dead are not raised, then Christ has not been raised. If Christ has not been raised, your faith is futile and you are still in your sins. Then those also who have died in Christ have perished. If for this life only we have hoped in Christ, we are of all people most to be pitied.

---

[15] Reinhold Niebuhr, *The Nature and Destiny of Man*, vol. 2 (New York: Charles Scribner's Sons, 1943), pp. 295-297. Cf. Reinhold Niebuhr, *Faith and History* (New York: Charles Scribner's Sons, 1949), p. 150.

But in fact Christ has been raised from the dead, the first fruits of those who have died (1 Cor. 15: 12-20).

How is the Christian to believe that her or his death does not annihilate *(zerstören)* everything, does not vanquish all hope and meaning? Upon two counts: God is *there* to overcome death. And in Jesus Christ, God *has* overcome death. Jesus Christ is the first fruits.

In *The Political Meaning of Christianity* Glenn Tinder applies to the terrifying question before us what he calls "prophetic spirituality," an effort "to enter fully into the truth . . . of our journey through history into eternity." Since "my destiny is universally human," it follows that "prophetic spirituality is fundamentally political as well as personal – aimed at discerning, in the necessities and responsibilities that shape my life, the meaning of history."

> The principle that we are strong only when we are weak, rich only when we are poor, alive only when we are dead, gives Christian hope and the Christian way of living in history the distinctive character that marks off Christian radicalism from secular radicalism. We do not command the future, in the Christian vision, but receive it from the hands of God, and we receive it only by giving up all pretensions of historical sovereignty, in dying. And the future given to us is not confined to the world or describable in terms of worldly realities; the things "God has prepared for those who love him" are things "no eye has seen, nor ear heard, nor the heart of man conceived" [1 Cor. 2:9, *RSV*; cf. Isa. 64:4; 65:17] . . . . A radicalism formed by so paradoxical a faith is drastically different from secular radicalism. It is prepared to encounter limitations and suffer defeat; it is impelled by faith rather than self-confidence; in a word – a word that will damn it in the eyes of secular radicals – it is otherworldly. That otherworldliness carries political dangers must be admitted; for Christians, defeat does not bring despair, and the result may be that they are more willing than they should be to suffer defeat. But otherworldliness may have consequences more favorable to a radical posture. It may give rise to a hope, free of arrogance, that cannot be defeated.[16]

Death for Death

Only one counteraction to death is available: the God who, as vouchsafed in our brief allusion to the Trinity, "always has been and always will be," the One who, present with God's people in life, is yet present with them in death, the One who undergoes death in the

---

[16]Glenn Tinder, *The Political Meaning of Christianity* (Baton Rouge-London: Louisiana State University Press, 1989), pp. 229, 231-232. Consult also Monika K. Hellwig, *What Are They Saying About Death and Christian Hope?* (New York: Paulist Press, 1978); and *Word & World* 11, 1 (1991), special number on "Death and Resurrection."

death of the Son of God, the One who stands by God's people as Friend after everything else is gone.

To counteract death is assuring and noble, but there is one thing more: "The last enemy to be *destroyed* is death" (I Cor. 15:26). Faith and love join hope in the affirmation that in the end death is itself sentenced to death:

> He will swallow up death forever, and the Lord God will wipe away tears from all faces, and the reproach of his people he will take away from all the earth; for the Lord has spoken (Isa. 25:8, *RSV*).

> I heard a great voice from the throne saying, "Behold the dwelling of God is among mortals. He will dwell with them, and they shall be his people, and God himself will be with them; he will wipe away every tear from their eyes, and death shall be no more, neither shall there be mourning nor crying nor pain any more, for the former things have passed away" (Rev. 21:3-4, *RSV, NRSV*).

With the death of death, Life *(haim)* remains – to be, to be joyful, to celebrate. One day our hearts will rejoice, and no one will take our joy from us. We will be made safe within the laughter of God.[17]

---

[17]Consult Gerhard Staguhn, *God's Laughter: Man and His Cosmos*, trans. Steve Lake and Caroline Mähl (New York: HarperCollins, 1992).

For Further Reading

The relative shortness of the present book may be partially balanced by this reading list. Additional sources of pertinence are found among the notes to the several chapters.

Becker, Ernest. *The Denial of Death.* New York: Free Press, 1973.

_____. *Escape From Evil.* New York: Free Press, 1975.

Birnbaum, David. *God and Evil: A Unified Theodicy/Theology/Philosophy.* Hoboken: Ktav Publishing House, 1989.

Blue, Lionel. *To Heaven With Scribes and Pharisees.* New York: Oxford University Press, 1976.

Boesak, Allan. *Farewell to Innocence: A Socio-ethical Study in Black Power.* Maryknoll NY: Orbis Books, 1977.

Brandon, S. G. F. *The Judgment of the Dead: The Idea of Life After Death in the Major Religions.* New York: Charles Scribner's Sons, 1967.

Carr, Anne E. *Transforming Grace: Christian Tradition and Women's Experience.* San Francisco: Harper & Row, 1988.

Chopp, Rebecca S. *The Power to Speak: Feminism, Language, God.* New York: Crossroad, 1989.

Cobb, John B., Jr. *Matters of Life and Death.* Louisville: Westminster/John Knox Press, 1991.

Cobb, John B., Jr. and Christopher Ives, eds. *The Emptying God: A Buddhist-Jewish-Christian Conversation.* Maryknoll NY: Orbis Books, 1990.

Cohen, Arthur A. *The Tremendum: A Theological Interpretation of the Holocaust.* New York: Crossroad, 1981.

Coles, Robert. *The Spiritual Life of Children*. Boston: Houghton Mifflin, 1990.

Cone, James. *A Black Theology of Liberation*, 2nd ed. Maryknoll NY: Orbis Books, 1986.

Cox, Harvey. *The Feast of Fools: A Theological Essay on Festivity and Fantasy*. Cambridge: Harvard University Press, 1969.

_____. *Many Mansions: A Christian's Encounter with Other Faiths*. Boston: Beacon Press, 1988.

Culbertson, Philip. *New Adam: The Future of Male Spirituality*. Minneapolis: Fortress Press, 1992.

Davidson, James D., C. Lincoln Johnson, and Alan K. Mock, eds. *Faith and Social Ministry: Ten Christian Perspectives*. Chicago: Loyola University Press, 1990.

Davies, Christie. *Ethnic Humor Around the world: A Comparative Analysis*. Bloomington: Indiana University Press, 1990.

Eckardt, Alice L., and A. Roy Eckardt. *Long Night's Journey Into Day: A Revised Retrospective on the Holocaust*. Detroit: Wayne State University Press; Oxford: Pergamon Press, 1988.

Eckardt, A. Roy. *Black-Woman-Jew: Three Wars for Human Liberation*. Bloomington: Indiana University Press, 1989.

_____. *Elder and Younger Brothers: The Encounter of Jews and Christians*. New York: Charles Scribner's Sons, 1967; Schocken Books, 1973.

_____. *For Righteousness' Sake: Contemporary Moral Philosophies*. Bloomington: Indiana University Press, 1987.

_____. *How To Tell God From the Devil: On the Way to Comedy* (forthcoming).

_____. *Jews and Christians: The Contemporary Meeting*. Bloomington: Indiana University Press, 1986.

_____. *Reclaiming the Jesus of History: Christology Today*. Minneapolis: Fortress Press, 1992.

_____. *Sitting in the Earth and Laughing: A Handbook of Humor*. New Brunswick-London: Transaction, Rutgers-The State University of New Jersey, 1992.

Erasmus, Desiderius. *Praise of Folly*, trans John Wilson. Ann Arbor: University of Michigan Press, 1958.

Fackenheim, Emil L. *To Mend the World: Foundations of Post-Holocaust Thought.* New York: Schocken Books, 1989.

Farley, Wendy. *Tragic Vision and Divine Compassion: A Contemporary Theodicy.* Louisville: Westminster/John Knox Press, 1990.

Fasching, Darrell J. *Narrative Theology After Auschwitz: From Alienation to Ethics.* Minneapolis: Fortress Press, 1992.

Fiorenza, Francis Schüssler, and John P. Galvin, eds. *Systematic Theology: Roman Catholic Perspectives*, 2 vols. Minneapolis: Fortress Press, 1991.

Green, Michael. *I Believe in Satan's Downfall.* London: Hodder & Stoughton, 1981.

Hampson, Daphne. *Theology and Feminism.* Oxford: Basil Blackwell, 1990.

Hawking, Stephen. *A Brief History of Time: From the Big Bang to Black Holes.* New York: Bantam Books, 1988.

Hellwig, Monika K. *What Are They Saying About Death and Christian Hope?* New York: Paulist Press, 1978.

Heschel, Abraham Joshua. *The Prophets*, 2 vols. New York: Harper Colophon Books, 1969, 1975.

Hyers, Conrad. *The Comic Vision and the Christian Faith: A Celebration of Life and Laughter.* New York: Pilgrim Press, 1981.

Johnson, Elizabeth A. *She Who Is: The Mystery of God in Feminist Theological Discourse.* New York: Crossroad, 1993.

Knitter, Paul F. *No Other Name? A Critical Survey of Christian Attitudes Toward the World Religions.* Maryknoll NY: Orbis Books, 1985.

Küng, Hans. *On Being A Christian*, trans. Edward Quinn. New York: Pocket Books, 1976.

Laytner, Anson. *Arguing With God: A Jewish Tradition.* Northvale NJ-London: Jason Aronson, 1990.

Levenson, Jon D. *Creation and the Persistence of Evil: The Jewish Drama of Divine Omnipotence.* San Francisco: Harper & Row, 1988.

Lewis, C. S. *The Screwtape Letters.* London: Collins, 1977.

McFague, Sallie. *Models of God: Theology for an Ecological Nuclear Age.* Philadelphia: Fortress Press, 1987.

Macquarrie, John. *Jesus Christ in Modern Thought.* London: SCM Press; Philadelphia: Trinity Press International, 1990.

_____. *Principles of Christian Theology*, 2nd ed. New York: Charles Scribner's Sons, 1977.

Maduro, Otto, ed. *Judaism, Christianity and Liberation: An Agenda for Dialogue*. Maryknoll NY: Orbis Books, 1991.

Metz, Johann Baptist, and Jean-Pierre Jossua, eds. *"You Have Sorrow Now, But Your Hearts Will Rejoice." Concilium* (New Series) 5, 10 (May 1974).

Moltmann, Jürgen. *The Crucified God: The Cross of Christ as the Foundation and Criticism of Christian Theology*, trans. R. A. Wilson and John Bowden. New York: Harper & Row, 1974.

_____. *The Way of Jesus Christ: Christology in Messianic Dimensions*, trans. Margaret Kohl. San Francisco: HarperSanFrancisco, 1990.

Nicholls, William. *Christian Antisemitism: A History of Hate*. Northvale NJ-London: Jason Aronson, 1993.

Niebuhr, H. Richard. *Faith on Earth: An Inquiry into the Structure of Human Faith*, ed. Richard R. Niebuhr. New Haven-London: Yale University Press, 1989.

_____. *Radical Monotheism and Western Culture*. New York: Harper & Brothers, 1960.

_____. *The Responsible Self: An Essay in Christian Moral Philosophy*. San Francisco: Harper & Row, 1978.

Niebuhr, Reinhold. *The Nature and Destiny of Man: A Christian Interpretation*, 2 vols. New York: Charles Scribner's Sons, 1941, 1943.

_____. *The Self and the Dramas of History*. New York: Charles Scribner's Sons, 1955.

Oden, Thomas C. *Systematic Theology*, 2 vols. New York: Harper & Row, 1981, 1989.

Osten-Sacken, Peter von der. *Christian-Jewish Dialogue: Theological Foundations*, trans. Margaret Kohl. Philadelphia: Fortress Press, 1986.

Plaskow, Judith. *Standing Again at Sinai: Judaism from a Feminist Perspective*. San Francisco: Harper & Row, 1991.

Saward, John. *Perfect Fools: Folly for Christ's Sake in Catholic and Orthodox Spirituality*. New York: Oxford University Press, 1980.

Staguhn, Gerhard. *God's Laughter: Man and His Cosmos*, trans. Steve Lake and Caroline Mähl. New York: HarperCollins, 1992.

Tanner, Kathryn. *The Politics of God: Christian Theologies and Social Justice.* Minneapolis: Fortress Press, 1992.

Thielicke, Helmut. *Theological Ethics,* 2 vols., ed. William H. Press, 1966, 1969.

Thistlethwaite, Susan Brooks, and Mary Potter Engels, eds. *Lift Every Voice: Constructing Christian Theologies from the Underside.* San Francisco: Harper & Row, 1990.

Tillich, Paul. *The Courage To Be.* New Haven: Yale University Press, 1952.

_____. *Dynamics of Faith.* New York: Harper & Brothers, 1957.

_____. *Systematic Theology,* 3 vols. Chicago: University of Chicago Press, 1951, 1957, 1963.

Tinder, Glenn. *The Political Meaning of Christianity: An Interpretation.* Baton Rouge-London: Louisiana State University Press, 1989.

Van Buren, Paul M. *A Christian Theology of the People Israel,* Part II - *A Theology of the Jewish-Christian Reality.* New York: Seabury Press, 1983.

Welch, Sharon D. *A Feminist Ethic of Risk.* Minneapolis: Fortress Press, 1989.

Williamson, Clark, ed. *A Mutual Witness: Toward Critical Solidarity Between Jews & Christians.* St. Louis: Chalice Press, 1992.

Willimon, William H., compiler. *And the Laugh Shall Be First: A Treasury of Religious Humor.* Nashville: Abingdon Press, 1986.

_____, compiler. *Last Laugh.* Nashville: Abingdon Press, 1991.

Winter, Gibson. *Liberating Creation: Foundations of Religious Social Ethics.* New York: Crossroad, 1981.

Wyschogrod, Michael. *The Body of Faith: God in the People Israel.* San Francisco: Harper & Row, 1989.

Index to Biblical References

General Index

South Florida Studies in the History of Judaism

South Florida Academic Commentary Series

The Talmud of Babylonia, An Academic Commentary

South Florida-Rochester-Saint Louis
Studies on Religion and the Social Order

South Florida International Studies in
Formative Christianity and Judaism

Books by A. Roy Eckardt

Christianity and the Children of Israel
The Surge of Piety in America
Elder and Younger Brothers
The Theologian at Work (editor)
Christianity in Israel (editor)
Your People, My People
Jews and Christians
For Righteousness' Sake
Black-Woman-Jew
Reclaiming the Jesus of History
Sitting in the Earth and Laughing
Collecting Myself, ed. Alice L. Eckardt
No Longer Aliens, No Longer Strangers
How To Tell God From the Devil (forthcoming)
On the Way to Death (forthcoming)

By Alice L. Eckardt and A. Roy Eckardt

Encounter With Israel
Long Night's Journey Into Day